EARTH SHATTERING EVENTS

WRITTEN BY ROBIN JACOBS
ILLUSTRATED BY SOPHIE WILLIAMS

CONTENTS

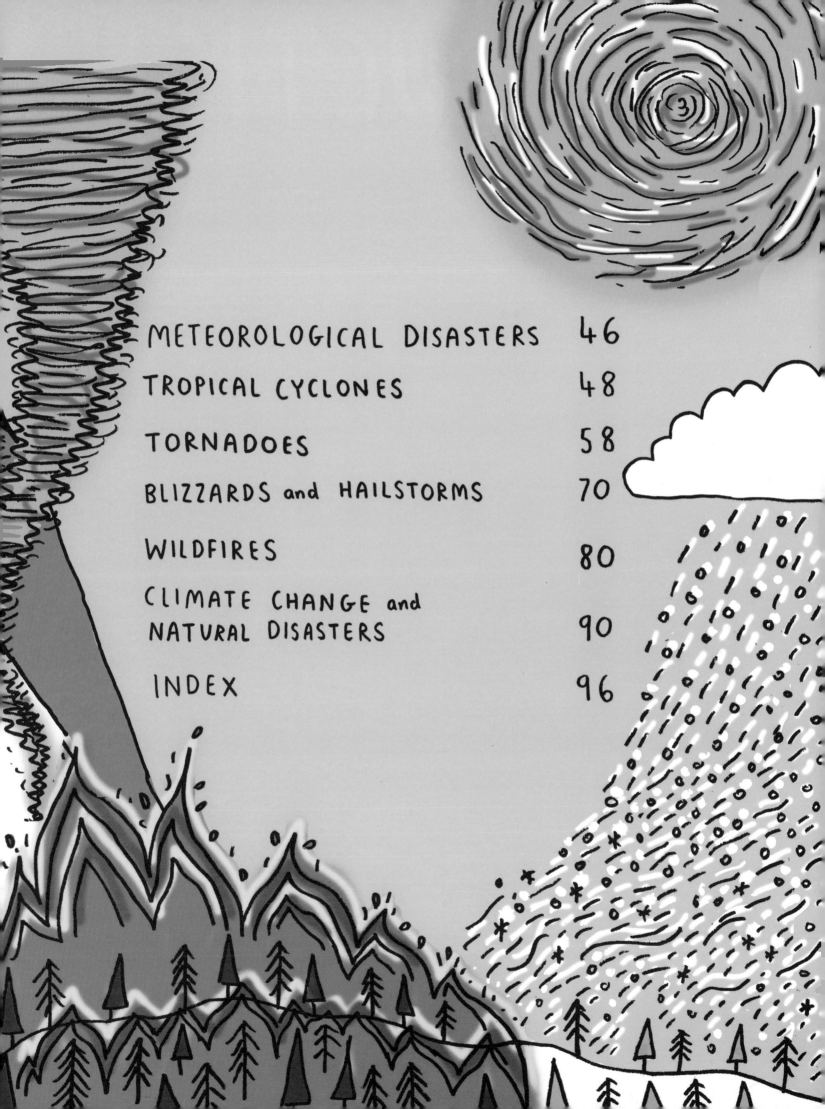

INTRODUCTION

Our species, Homo sapiens, or humans, takes its domination of the planet for granted. We strip the planet of its resources to grow our crops, feed our livestock, fuel our cars and make the millions of products that have become part of our lifestyles.

But every so often, the planet reminds us who's boss. The ground beneath our feet trembles and shakes and even ruptures. Great waves or storms sweep into our pleasant beach resorts, leaving behind nothing but rubble. Eruptions of liquid stone spew forth from volcanoes that for thousands of years seemed like nothing more than harmless mountains.

A natural disaster refers to a catastrophic event that impacts upon humans. When a volcano erupts deep under the sea, we do not think of this as a disaster, but rather a natural phenomenon. To be a disaster, property must be damaged, communities destroyed and lives lost. Often, the people who are most affected by natural disasters are the most vulnerable; the ones who have no choice but to live in the danger zone, in ramshackle housing. The ones who cannot afford to buy in exported food or clean water when their water source gets contaminated or dries out. In developing countries, when infrastructure like roads or bridges are destroyed, it takes many years to repair them, and so the damage left behind often takes many decades to overcome.

And it is not just humans that are harmed by natural disasters. Changes in soil and water quality, scorched forests and changing coastlines can have a huge impact on ecosystems and the wildlife that inhabits them.

Natural disasters are becoming more frequent and more extreme as a result of climate change (see p. 90). It is ironic that those least responsible for climate change are the ones most affected.

In any given year, there may be two or three hundred large-scale disasters. Using modern technology, Scientists can predict events like blizzards, cyclones and other weather-related disasters, allowing the affected populations to evacuate or prepare, but some disasters like earthquakes, tsunamis, volcanic eruptions or wildfires have very short warning times, and the results can be catastrophic.

These disasters demonstrate the immense power of nature. In their terrifying, destructive force, they make us realise how tiny and insignificant we are in the context of Earth's long, rich history. They remind us that we must always respect and look after this most special of planets.

Earth's outer layer (the lithosphere) is made up of large plates of rock called tectonic plates that float on top of a layer of thick molten rock called magma. We think of the ground beneath us as sturdy and secure. We use terms like 'down to earth' and 'grounded' to refer to something dependable and permanent. But in fact the tectonic plates are in constant motion, adjusting themselves to the flow of magma beneath them.

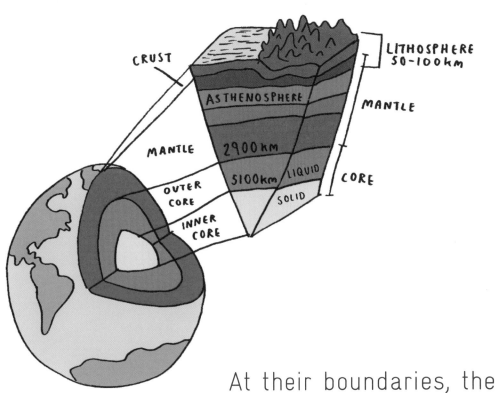

CONVERGENT.

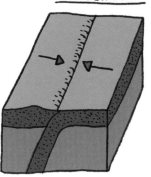

DIVERGENT.

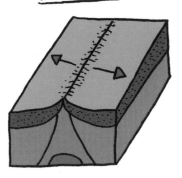

TRANSFORM.

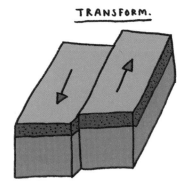

At their boundaries, the plates interact; pushing together, pulling away or sliding past each other. These interactions cause land to be created, earthquakes to happen, land to buckle into mountains and volcanoes to form and erupt.

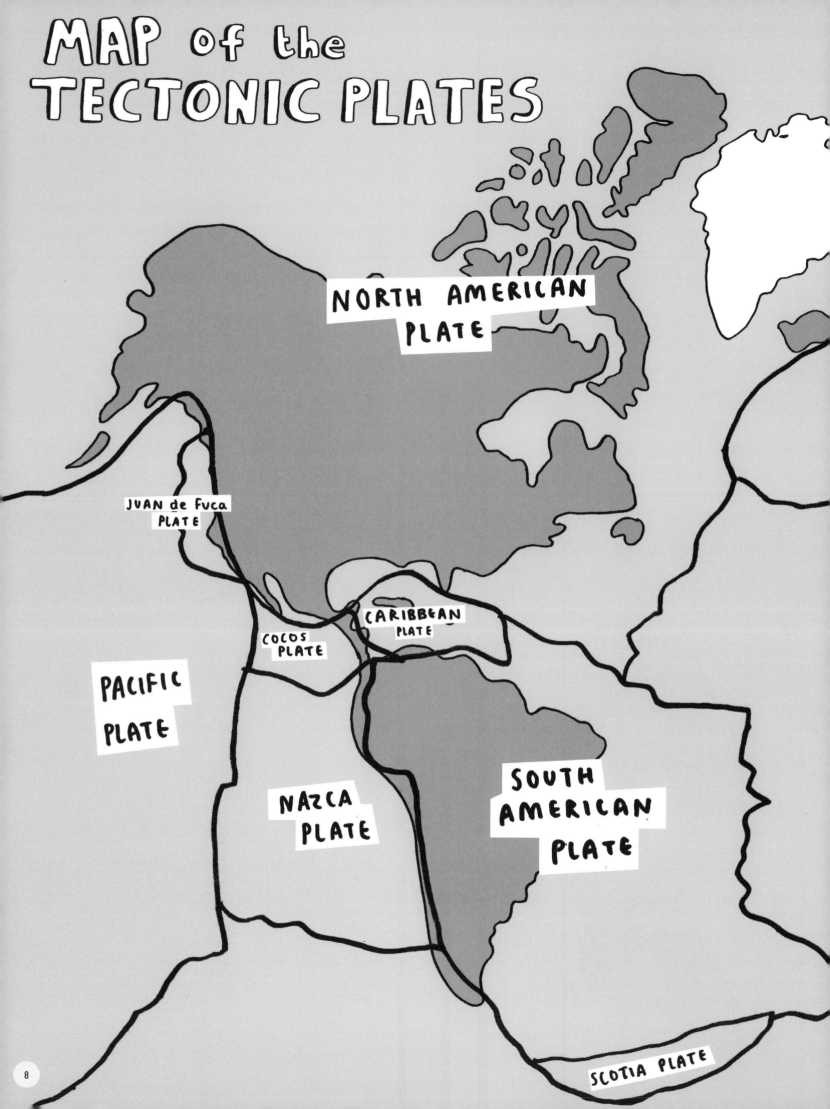

MAP of the TECTONIC PLATES

NORTH AMERICAN PLATE

JUAN de Fuca PLATE

CARIBBEAN PLATE

COCOS PLATE

PACIFIC PLATE

NAZCA PLATE

SOUTH AMERICAN PLATE

SCOTIA PLATE

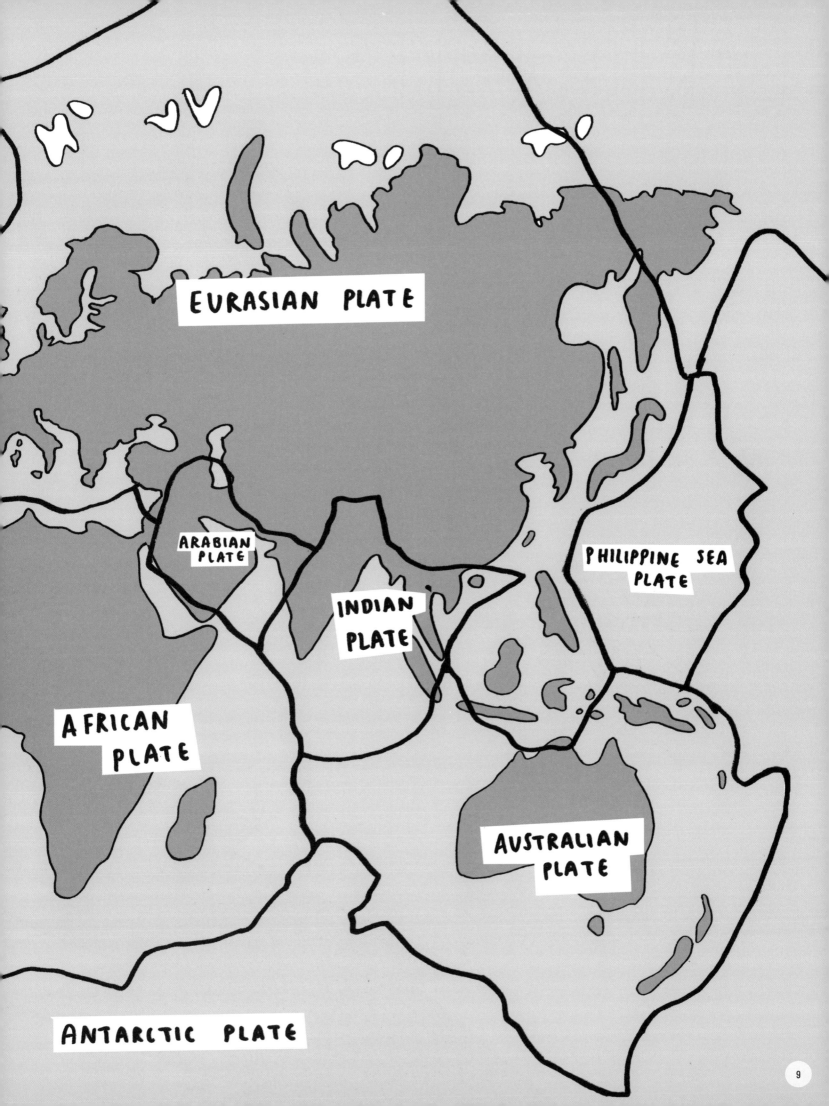

EARTHQUAKES

A fault is a thin zone of crushed rock, separating two tectonic plates. When the plates push under or past each other, pressure builds up along the fault, until eventually the plates slip and an earthquake occurs.

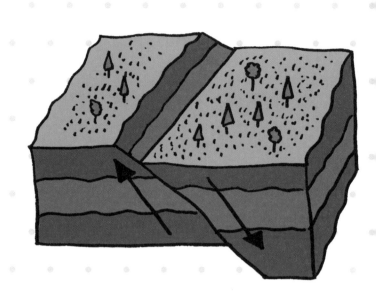

It's a bit like snapping your fingers. You push your fingers together and sideways. Friction stops them from moving, until the force of the sideways push overcomes it, and your fingers move suddenly, releasing energy in the form of soundwaves.

The same thing happens in an earthquake. The tectonic plates push against each other as they try to move past. Eventually, they slip suddenly, releasing energy in the form of seismic waves that travel through the rock, causing the earth to shake.

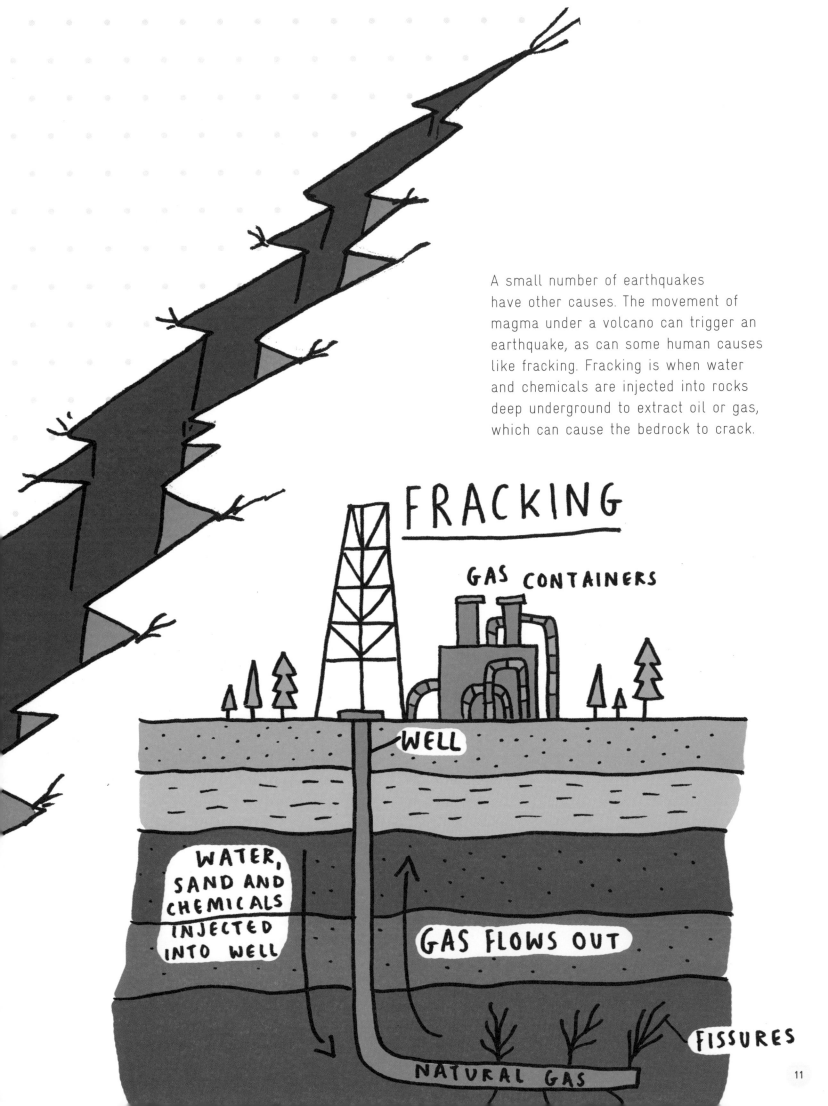

A small number of earthquakes have other causes. The movement of magma under a volcano can trigger an earthquake, as can some human causes like fracking. Fracking is when water and chemicals are injected into rocks deep underground to extract oil or gas, which can cause the bedrock to crack.

FRACKING

GAS CONTAINERS

WELL

WATER, SAND AND CHEMICALS INJECTED INTO WELL

GAS FLOWS OUT

FISSURES

NATURAL GAS

11

EARTHQUAKE MYTHS

In Hindu mythology, Earth is held in place by eight gigantic elephants balanced on the back of turtle, which stands on a coiled up snake. If any of these animals shift, an earthquake occurs.

In Ancient Greece, people believed that Poseidon, god of the sea, caused earthquakes by striking the ground with his trident in a fit of rage. He was nicknamed 'Earth Shaker'.

In Japanese mythology it is said that earthquakes are caused by a giant, underground-dwelling catfish called Namazu. Namazu is guarded by the god Kashima, but when Kashima lets his guard down, Namazu thrashes around, causing the earth to shake.

EARTHQUAKE FACTS

Around 500,000 detectable earthquakes happen annually. In Japan alone, there are at least 1,500 earthquakes every year – around two or three per day! Most of those are so tiny that nobody can feel them.

Approximately 100 earthquakes per year are big enough to cause damage to properties, and earthquakes with a magnitude of 8 and up (see p. 15) occur about once a year. 80 percent of the world's most powerful earthquakes happen in the horseshoe-shaped belt around the edges of the Pacific Plate, known as the 'Ring of Fire' (see p. 29).

Most earthquakes last about one minute. The longest recorded earthquake lasted for ten minutes.

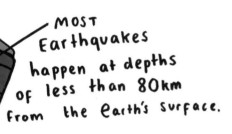

MOST Earthquakes happen at depths of less than 80km from the Earth's surface.

Often, before and after a large earthquake, there will be smaller earthquakes. These are called foreshocks and aftershocks. Aftershocks are unpredictable and very dangerous, as they can cause the collapse of buildings that were damaged in the main shock. They can also cause mudslides and land collapse.

MEASURING EARTHQUAKES

Shock waves from an earthquake travel through the ground and are called seismic waves. Seismologists are people who study earthquakes.

The seismic waves spread out from the focus point; the point at which the earthquake started. The land above this point is called the epicentre. Most earthquake damage happens in and around the epicentre.

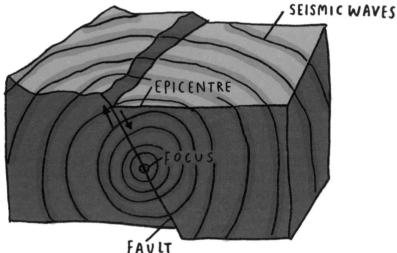

SEISMIC WAVES

EPICENTRE

FOCUS

FAULT

A seismograph records an earthquake's shockwaves, allowing scientists to measure its intensity.

The Richter scale measures earthquakes based on the amount of energy released. The Moment Magnitude scale (MMS) is similar, but takes into account the geometry of the fault as well as the energy released. It is more accurate than the Richter scale, and is most commonly used for measuring large earthquakes.

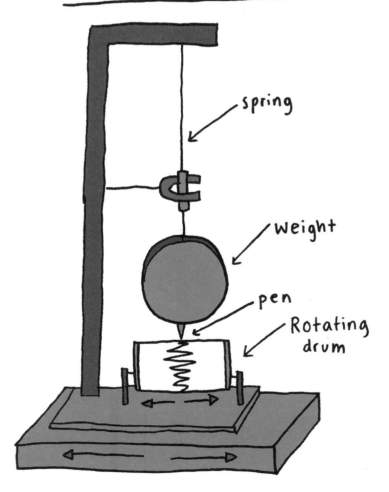

SEISMOGRAPH

spring

weight

pen

Rotating drum

MOMENT MAGNITUDE SCALE

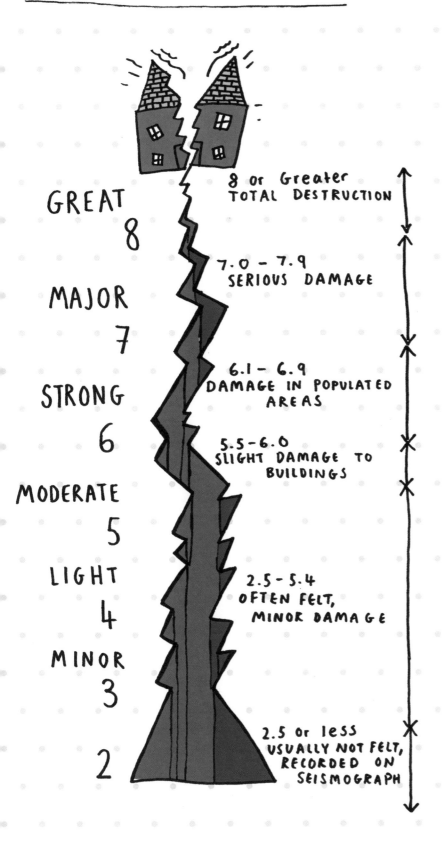

GREAT
8

MAJOR
7

STRONG
6

MODERATE
5

LIGHT
4

MINOR
3

2

8 or Greater
TOTAL DESTRUCTION

7.0 – 7.9
SERIOUS DAMAGE

6.1 – 6.9
DAMAGE IN POPULATED
AREAS

5.5 – 6.0
SLIGHT DAMAGE TO
BUILDINGS

2.5 – 5.4
OFTEN FELT,
MINOR DAMAGE

2.5 or less
USUALLY NOT FELT,
RECORDED ON
SEISMOGRAPH

WHAT TO DO IN AN EARTHQUAKE

DROP!

If you are indoors, shelter under a table or bench. Hold on to it firmly and if it moves, move with it. Stay away from windows, bookcases, hanging objects or tall, heavy furniture.

COVER!

If you are outdoors, stay away from tall buildings, streetlamps and power lines.

HOLD ON!

When all shaking stops, head for the exit. Never use the lift – always use stairs, and be prepared for possible aftershocks.

EFFECTS OF EARTHQUAKES

There is almost no warning before an earthquake occurs. Scientists can predict the probability of an earthquake, but not the actual event. This means that the impact can be devastating.

GROUND RUPTURE
Earthquakes can cause geographical changes along fault lines. Land can rise or drop dramatically. Ground rupture is when the land visibly breaks along the line of the fault.

DESTRUCTION
A large earthquake will cause a lot of damage to man-made structures such as buildings, roads and bridges. The amount of damage caused depends on the type of construction used. In 1909, an earthquake in Messina in Italy caused nearly all the structures in the villages to collapse, killing more than 100,000 people, whereas a bigger earthquake in 1906 in San Francisco only killed 700 people, because the buildings were more durable.

SAN FRANCISCO

ITALY

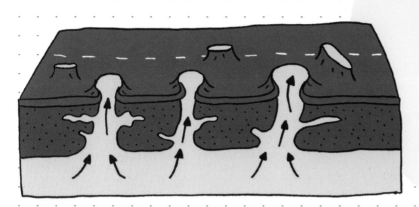

LIQUEFACTION
Earthquakes can cause the groundwater to rise, mixing with the soil above, and turning solid ground into something like quicksand, so that buildings can sink or tip over. This effect is called 'liquefaction'.

FIRES are common directly after earthquakes, as broken power and gas lines are major fire hazards. Floods can result from broken dams.

TSUNAMIS are caused by the displacement of water in the ocean, after an earthquake. These huge waves can be massively destructive (see pp. 20–27).

THE BIGGEST AND THE WORST

THE GREAT ALASKAN EARTHQUAKE, USA, 1964

VALDIVIA, CHILE, 1960

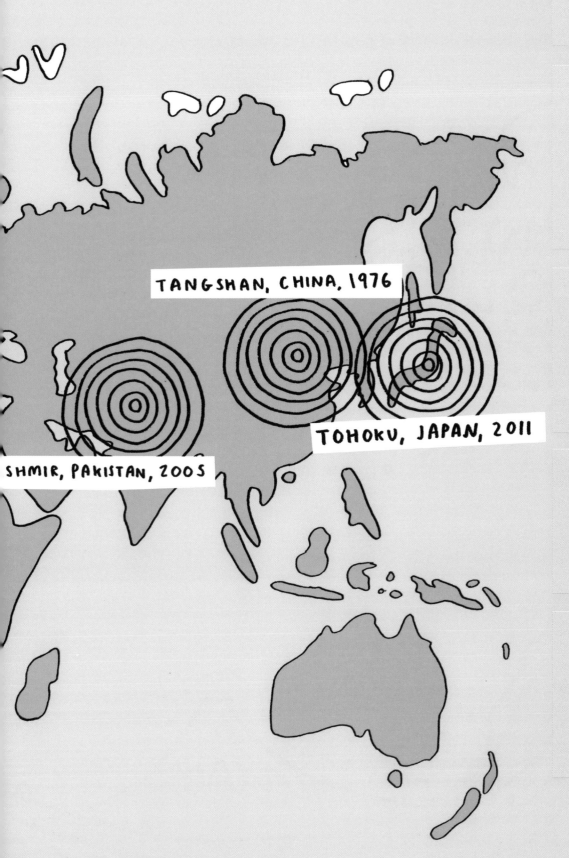

Valdivia, Chile / 22nd May 1960

The biggest earthquake ever recorded, measuring 9.4. It caused major damage as well as triggering landslides, flooding and tsunamis, leading to the deaths of 4,000 people.

Tohoku, Japan / 11th March 2011

A magnitude 9 earthquake off the coast of Japan that caused the collapse of 121,000 buildings, including a nuclear power plant. The earthquake was so powerful that it moved the main island of Japan 2.4 m to the east!

The Great Alaskan Earthquake, USA / 27th March 1964

The second most powerful earthquake ever recorded at 9.2. It caused environmental damage, but little else as the area is sparsely populated.

Kashmir and Pakistan / 8th October 2005

A 7.6 magnitude earthquake that hit a poor, densely populated area, causing thousands of buildings to collapse and the deaths of 80,000 people.

Tangshan, China / 28th July 1976

This 7.6 magnitude earthquake hit the city of Tangshan, and pretty much wiped it out. 85 percent of the buildings, roads and bridges were destroyed and at least 242,000 people were killed.

TANGSHAN, CHINA, 1976

TOHOKU, JAPAN, 2011

SHMIR, PAKISTAN, 2005

TSUNAMIS

Tsunamis are vast waves that speed across the ocean, causing terrible damage when they reach the shore. The word tsunami means 'harbour wave' in Japanese.

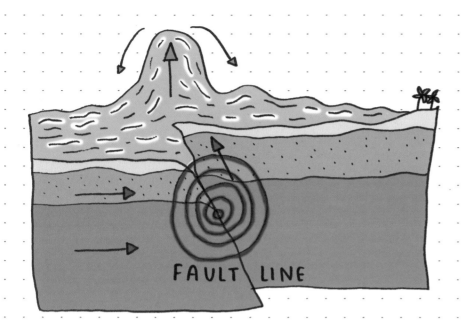

FAULT LINE

WHAT CAUSES A TSUNAMI?

A tsunami is caused by a displacement of water, often as a result of an earthquake, but sometimes as a result of a volcano, an underwater landslide or a meteorite.

If an earthquake lifts or drops part of the ocean floor, the water above rises in enormous waves.

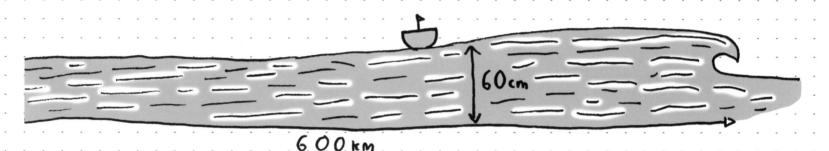

60cm

600 km

The waves ripple out from the point at which the water moved. They are very long waves, stretching for up to 600 km, but they are low, with crests only 30–60 cm high. This makes them very hard to detect. A person sailing on a tsunami wave in the deep ocean would only notice a gentle rise and fall.

The waves travel very fast – up to 800 km per hour – that's as fast as a jet plane! As the waves approach the coast, friction with the ocean floor causes the length of the waves shorten and their height to rise very quickly. Within ten minutes, the coastal waters can rise as high as 35 m.

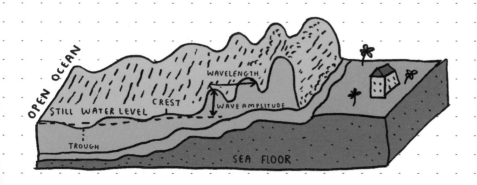

OPEN OCEAN
STILL WATER LEVEL
CREST
WAVELENGTH
WAVE AMPLITUDE
TROUGH
SEA FLOOR

WHAT HAPPENS?

If the wave hits the shore trough-first, it causes a vacuum effect called 'drawback'. The sea is drawn back from the shore, leaving fish and other animals flopping on the seabed.

A few minutes later, a vast wall of water travelling at around 150 km/h blasts the shore; uprooting trees, knocking over buildings and sometimes washing away entire beaches and coastal towns.

After the first wave, there are often more waves, sometimes with a gap of a few minutes, sometimes with an hour between waves. This is called a 'wave train'.

EFFECTS OF A TSUNAMI

Tsunamis cause damage in two ways; first when they hit, and afterwards when they drain away.

When a big tsunami hits, a wall of water smashes into coastal areas, followed by a huge rush of water that destroys everything in its path. Buildings, cars, trees and power lines can all be swept away as the tsunami travels inland. If a country is less developed and structures are not well built, the damage will be greater.

After the water has drained away, a lot of environmental damage may be left. Salt water can destroy rivers and freshwater lakes, causing loss of wildlife. Hazardous materials swept up in the water can contaminate soil.

Damage to sewage and waterways can lead to a lack of clean drinking water, causing diseases like cholera. Stagnant water left behind can bring other diseases like malaria.

TSUNAMI FACTS

There were two meteotsunami's in Lake Michigan in 1954 and 2018.

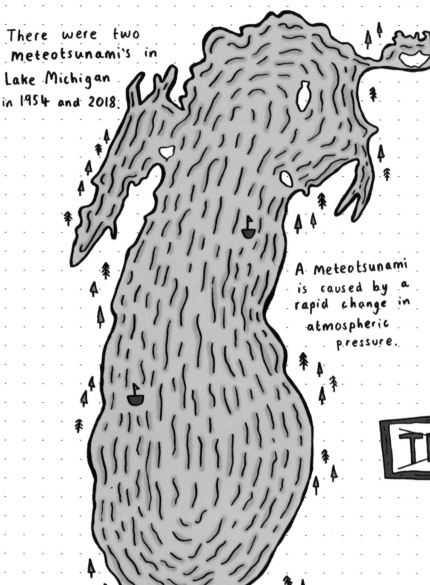

A Meteotsunami is caused by a rapid change in atmospheric pressure.

Around 80 percent of tsunamis occur in the Pacific Ocean. Japan and Indonesia are particularly vulnerable. However, they can happen anywhere, including Europe and the Mediterranean. They can even happen on inland lakes, in a phenomenon called meteotsunamis.

~~TIDAL WAVE~~

Tsunamis are sometimes called tidal waves, because they look like a swiftly rising tide. But in fact they have nothing to do with tides, so this name is incorrect.

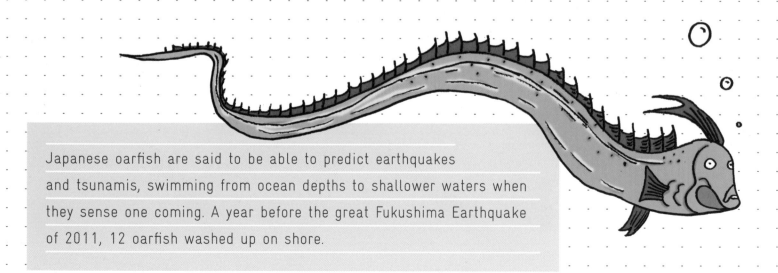

Japanese oarfish are said to be able to predict earthquakes and tsunamis, swimming from ocean depths to shallower waters when they sense one coming. A year before the great Fukushima Earthquake of 2011, 12 oarfish washed up on shore.

Scientists are still finding out about tsunamis. They don't know why some earthquakes cause tsunamis and others don't. This makes it hard to predict a tsunami.

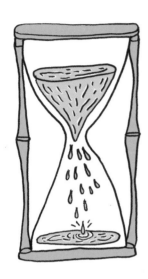

Scientists watch for changes in ocean levels and use devices to register the temperature and pressure of ocean water, as changes can be an indication of a tsunami. However there is often very little warning before a tsunami hits. Since 1850, it is estimated that around 430,000 lives have been lost in tsunamis.

WHAT TO DO IN A TSUNAMI

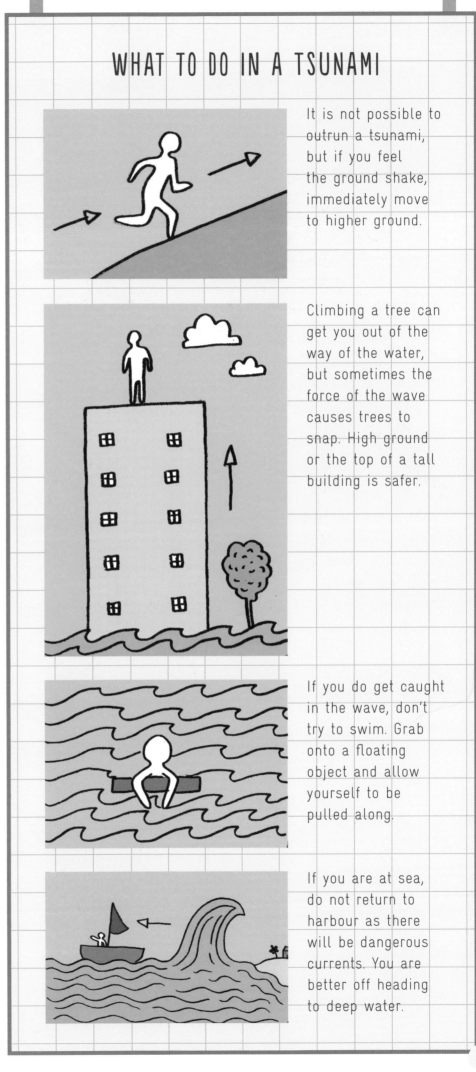

It is not possible to outrun a tsunami, but if you feel the ground shake, immediately move to higher ground.

Climbing a tree can get you out of the way of the water, but sometimes the force of the wave causes trees to snap. High ground or the top of a tall building is safer.

If you do get caught in the wave, don't try to swim. Grab onto a floating object and allow yourself to be pulled along.

If you are at sea, do not return to harbour as there will be dangerous currents. You are better off heading to deep water.

LITUYA BAY, ALASKA, 1958

Indian Ocean Tsunami / 26th December 2004

Following a huge earthquake off the coast of Indonesia, vast waves struck the coast of Sri Lanka, hours later hitting the Horn of Africa on the other side of the Indian Ocean. More than 200,000 people were killed in places as far away as Thailand, Malaysia, Bangladesh, and Somalia. It was the most destructive tsunami in history.

Japan Tsunami / 11th March 2011

A powerful earthquake caused a massive tsunami that devastated the eastern coast of Japan with waves as high as 10 m killing over 16,000 people. The city worst hit was Sendai.

Lituya Bay Tsunami / 9th July 1958

An earthquake triggered both a huge rockslide and the collapse of a glacier into a narrow Alaskan inlet. Although there was little loss to life, the resulting megawave reached 525 m – the highest ever recorded.

Sunda Strait Tsunami / 22nd December 2018

The eruption and partial collapse of the Little Krakatoa volcano caused a tsunami to hit 300 km of Indonesian coastline. There were no early warnings. 400 people died and 14,000 were injured.

JAPAN, 2011

SUNDA STRAIT, INDONESIA, 2018

INDIAN OCEAN, 2004

VOLCANOES

Volcanoes are mountains that open downwards to a pool of molten rock called magma.

Magma is lighter than rock, so rises towards the earth's surface. Gas bubbles cause pressure to build up inside the magma – like a soda bottle. As the pressure builds, magma can shoot out of the volcano in an eruption.

When magma leaves the volcano, it is called lava.

The word 'volcano' comes from the name of the Ancient Roman god of fire, Vulcan.

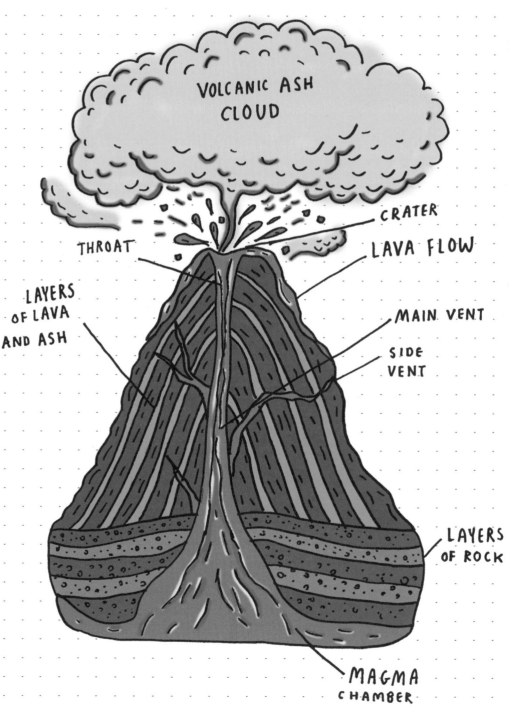

VOLCANIC ASH CLOUD

THROAT

CRATER

LAVA FLOW

LAYERS OF LAVA AND ASH

MAIN VENT

SIDE VENT

LAYERS OF ROCK

MAGMA CHAMBER

Volcanoes usually form at the meeting points of the tectonic plates. Where the plates are pushed under or away from each other, magma can force its way up through the cracks.

There are around 1,900 active volcanoes on earth. 90 percent of them can be found in the 'Ring of Fire', a 40,000 km² band under the Pacific Ocean.

RING of FIRE

TYPES OF VOLCANOES

OJOS del Salado, Andes

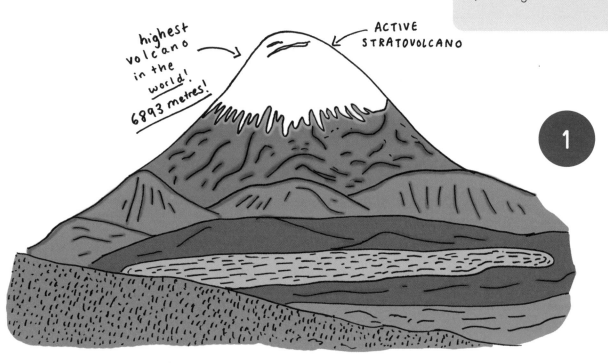

highest volcano in the world! 6893 metres!

ACTIVE STRATOVOLCANO

1 Stratovolcanoes

Stratovolcanoes are the tallest volcanoes. They are responsible for the biggest eruptions, fed by a number of small vents beneath the surface.

Ojos del Salado is an active stratovolcano in the Andes, straddling Chile and Argentina.

LAVA DOME

Some stratovolcanoes have lava domes in their craters. Lava domes are made of thick, slow-flowing lava that has cooled to create a big mound around the vent of a volcano.

2 Shield Volcanoes

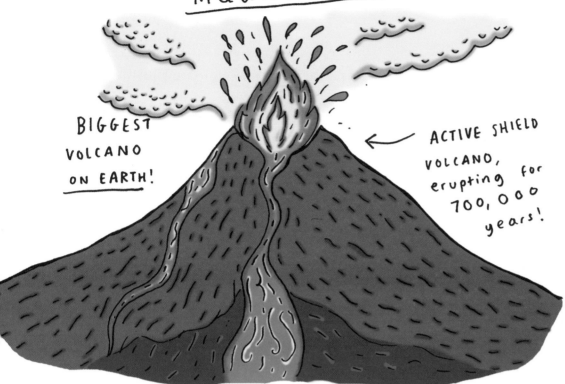

mauna Loa, Hawaii.

BIGGEST VOLCANO ON EARTH!

ACTIVE SHIELD VOLCANO, erupting for 700,000 years!

Shield volcanoes are wide and shallow with a flat summit. A stream of thin lava seeps steadily from the central vent, like overflowing liquid from a container. They experience frequent, but gentle eruptions.

Mauna Loa, in Hawaii, is an active shield volcano measuring 75,000 km³. It has been erupting for 700,000 years.

3 Cinder Cones

MOUNT SURIBACHI, JAPAN

DORMANT CINDER CONE

169m high!

Cinder cones are quite small. They push lava out of a single crater at the top.

Mount Suribachi in Japan is a dormant cinder cone. It measures 169 m high. Its name means 'grinding bowl'.

EFFECTS OF VOLCANOES

Around 350 million people live inside the danger zones of active volcanoes. This might seem a strange place to build your home, but the soil around volcanoes is often very fertile and good for farming.

A large eruption will cause devastation to the area around the volcano. Flows of lava reach 1170 ºC, burning everything in their path, whilst boulders of hardened lava rain down.

cough

choke

A thick layer of ash covers everything for miles around, killing livestock and causing breathing problems for many people.

If the ash and mud from an eruption is combined with heavy rainfall or melting snow, it can create fast-moving mudflows called lahars. Lahars can be extremely dangerous, burying entire villages.

A volcanic winter is caused when a huge eruption shoots a gas called sulphur dioxide into the atmosphere. When the gas breaks down into particles, these particles reflect sunlight away from the planet, cooling global temperatures by up to two degrees.

ERUPTIONS

There are six types of
volcanic eruption:

ICELANDIC

Lava seeps from long
cracks down the side of
the volcano.

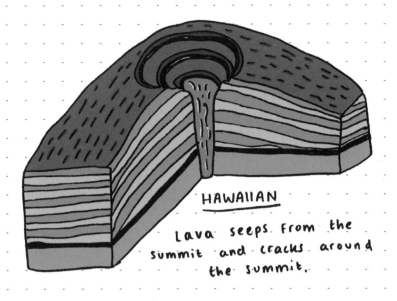

HAWAIIAN

Lava seeps from the
summit and cracks around
the summit.

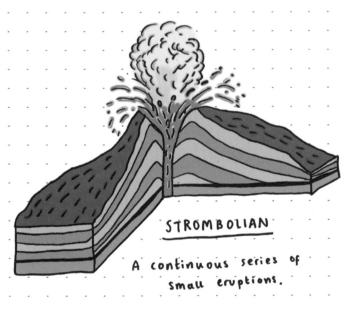

STROMBOLIAN

A continuous series of
small eruptions.

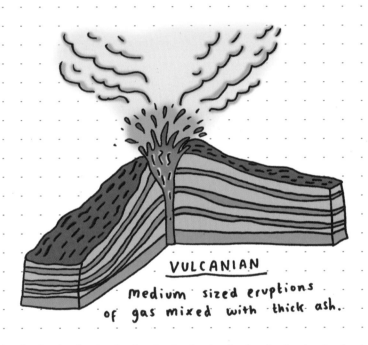

VULCANIAN

Medium sized eruptions
of gas mixed with thick ash.

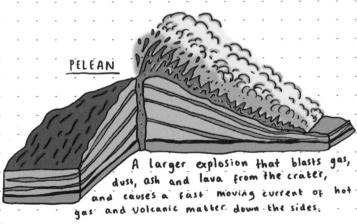

PELEAN

A larger explosion that blasts gas,
dust, ash and lava from the crater,
and causes a fast moving current of hot
gas and volcanic matter down the sides.

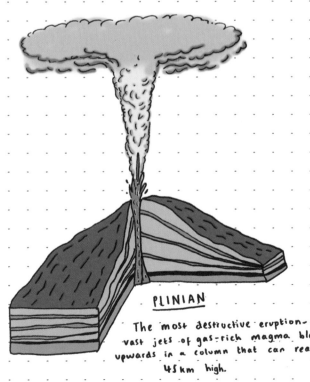

PLINIAN

The most destructive eruption-
vast jets of gas-rich magma blast
upwards in a column that can reach
45 km high.

People who study volcanoes are called vulcanologists.

They can tell when a volcano is likely to erupt because the temperature around the volcano starts to rise. Hundreds of little earthquakes indicate that magma is moving through the Earth's crust. The volcano starts to release gases with a high sulphur content.

THE VOLCANIC EXPLOSIVITY INDEX (VEI) is used to rank eruptions on a scale of 1 (weakest) to 8 (most powerful). A VEI 8 eruption only occurs when a 'supervolcano' erupts, once every 100,000 years or so, the last one being 26,000 years ago. The force of this eruption would be 100 times that of Krakatoa and its impact equivalent to that of an asteroid striking Earth.

WHAT TO DO IN A VOLCANO

If you are told to evacuate, wear long sleeved shirts and trousers and goggles. Do not wear contact lenses! Hold a damp cloth over your face.

Ash can clog up engines, so if you have to drive, stay below 50 km/h. Avoid rivers that might flood. Try to stay upwind of the volcano, as there will be less ash.

If you are told NOT to evacuate, close all windows and doors and block the chimney. Place damp rags at the base of every door. If the ash-fall is particularly heavy, you may need to climb onto your roof to sweep it away so that the roof doesn't collapse.

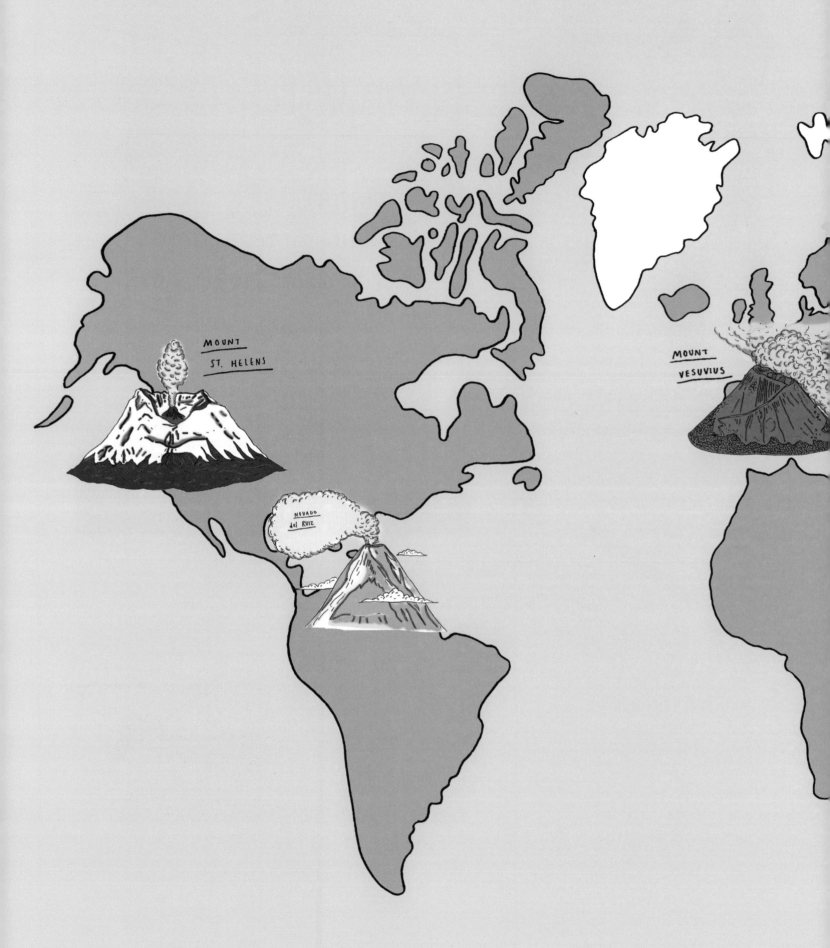

Mount Vesuvius, Italy / 79 AD / VEI 5

This eruption killed over 2,000 people and buried the city of Pompeii in a thick layer of ash. Rain then turned the ash into a kind of cement, so that centuries later archaeologists discovered a perfectly preserved example of life in Ancient Rome.

Krakatoa, Indonesia / 1883 / VEI 6

One of the most violent eruptions in history, generating the loudest sound ever heard and releasing 13,000 nuclear bombs worth of energy. 36,000 people were killed and tsunamis devastated many islands.

Mount St Helens, USA / 1980 / VEI 5

57 people were killed and over 200 km^2 of natural environment was destroyed in the most destructive volcano in US history.

Nevado del Ruiz, Colombia / 1985 / VEI 3

Although this was a small eruption, the mudflows that resulted buried the town of Armero, claiming 20,000 lives.

Mount Pinatubo, Philippines / 1991 / VEI 6

Mount Pinatubo was a dormant volcano that showed little signs of life, until a sudden eruption that killed 722 people and caused a volcanic winter that brought the Earth's temperatures down by 0.5 °C.

AVALANCHES

An avalanche is a big slab of snow that breaks away from a slope and travels quickly downhill, growing and gathering more snow as it cascades down.

WHAT CAUSES AN AVALANCHE?

When a big dump of snow is too heavy for the snowpack underneath it, a huge chunk can break away.

The snowpack is what we call the layers of snow that build up gradually over the winter. The structures of the ice crystals that make up the snowpack are affected by the weather. On a sunny day, for example, a layer of snow might melt and refreeze, causing changes in the ice crystals and making the snowpack slick or weak. A big dump of snow on top of a weak layer can then easily break away.

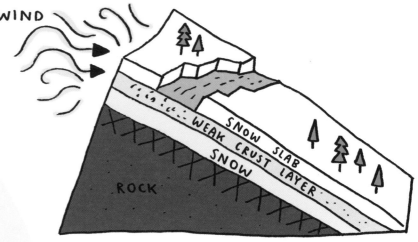

Avalanches are very common. In the Alps, there are around 10,000 avalanches a year. Most of these are small shiftings of loose snow, called sloughing, which are usually harmless.

A more dangerous phenomenon is a slab avalanche. This is when a big slab of snow breaks away and hurtles downhill, shattering like glass as it goes. A slab avalanche can reach speeds of 150 km/h within five seconds. Victims of these avalanches rarely survive.

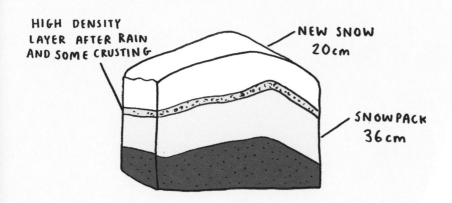

HIGH DENSITY LAYER AFTER RAIN AND SOME CRUSTING

NEW SNOW 20cm

SNOWPACK 36cm

TRIGGERING AN AVALANCHE

WIND

An avalanche is most likely to occur on a bare slope of 30-50 degrees. Steeper slopes will shed snow constantly, preventing a build-up. Gentler slopes don't have the gravitational pull to cause the snow to break away. Rocks and trees will anchor the snow.

The most dangerous conditions for an avalanche are a combination of heavy snowfall with strong winds. Wind can break down the ice crystals in the snow, so a slab can quickly form. Avalanches are most common in the 24 hours after a storm that dumps 30 cm or more of fresh snow.

If the conditions are right, it is very easy to trigger an avalanche. The movement of a skier or a snowmobile can easily loosen the snow. Spontaneous avalanches can happen with no trigger at all.

TYPES OF AVALANCHE

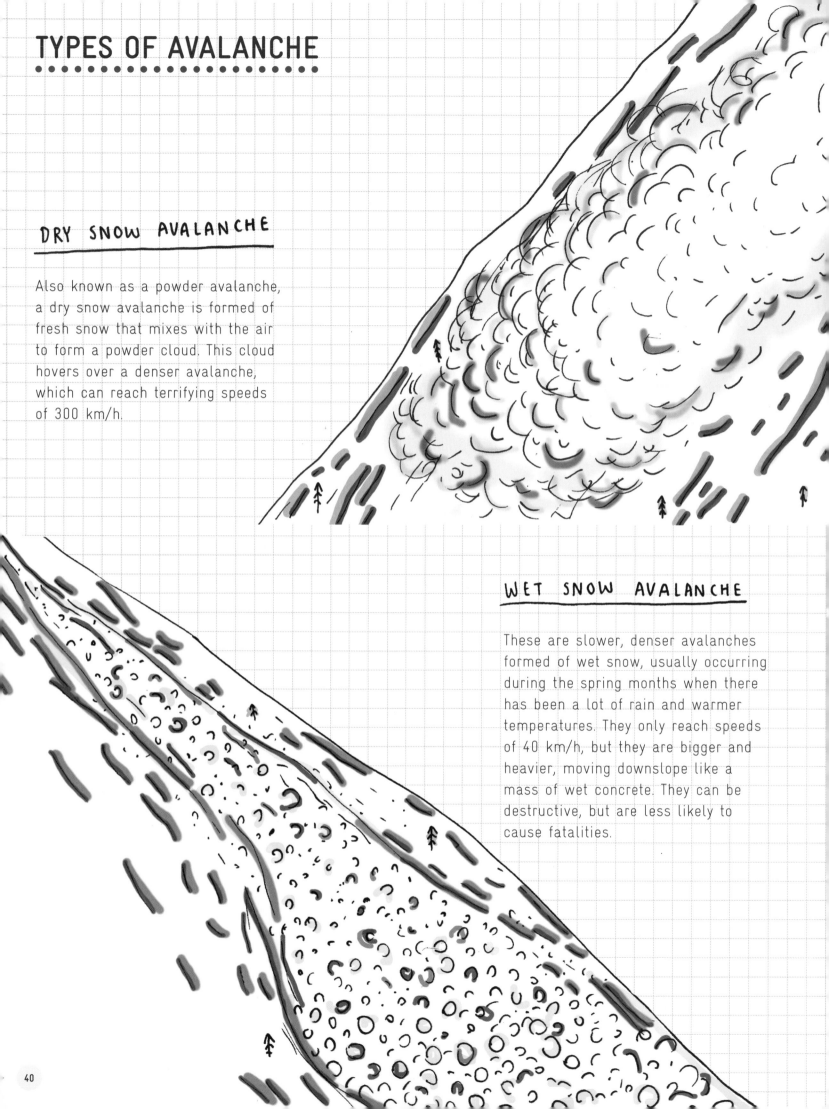

DRY SNOW AVALANCHE

Also known as a powder avalanche, a dry snow avalanche is formed of fresh snow that mixes with the air to form a powder cloud. This cloud hovers over a denser avalanche, which can reach terrifying speeds of 300 km/h.

WET SNOW AVALANCHE

These are slower, denser avalanches formed of wet snow, usually occurring during the spring months when there has been a lot of rain and warmer temperatures. They only reach speeds of 40 km/h, but they are bigger and heavier, moving downslope like a mass of wet concrete. They can be destructive, but are less likely to cause fatalities.

ANATOMY OF AN AVALANCHE

THE STARTING ZONE is the unstable area, where the snow starts its slide. This is usually quite high up on the slope.

THE AVALANCHE TRACK is the channel that the avalanche follows. Be careful of bare, chute-like slopes with pile-ups of snow at the bottom. This might indicate that avalanches have happened before and may happen again.

THE RUNOUT ZONE is where the snow and debris come to a stop. This is the area where victims are most likely to be buried.

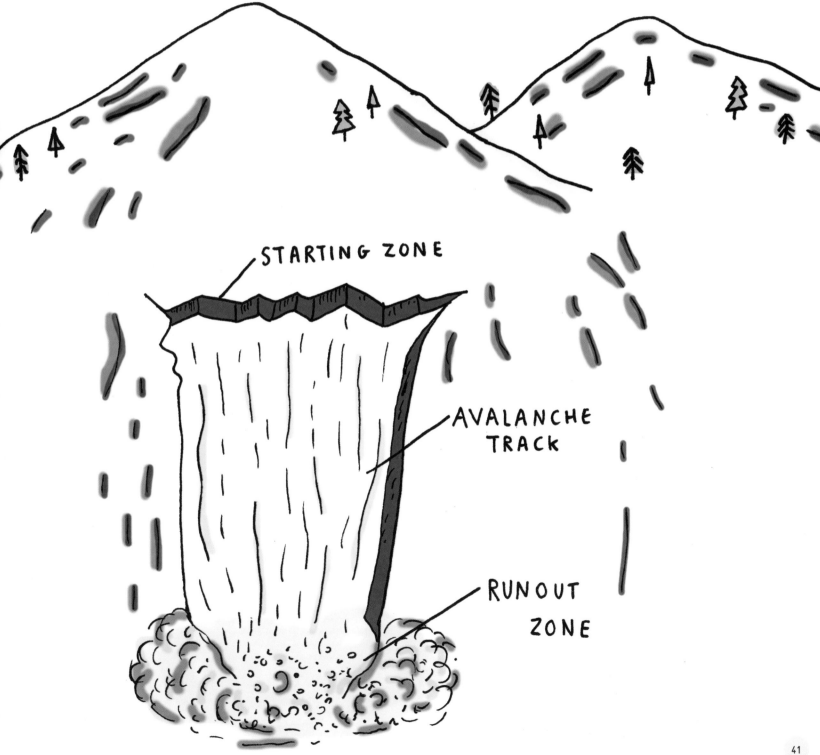

STARTING ZONE

AVALANCHE TRACK

RUNOUT ZONE

AVALANCHE PREVENTION

There are various ways that people can prevent avalanches. The simplest method is by travelling on the snowpack as it grows. This can be by walking, skiing or machine grooming. If the snowpack is kept dense, it is less likely to weaken.

Explosives are one way of controlling avalanches. By deliberately triggering small avalanches, it is less likely for a large avalanche to occur.

Another method of preventing avalanches is by using special fences to stop sliding snow.

STAY SAFE

As you walk or ski, keep an ear out for any hollow thumping noises. This might be an indication that there is a weaker layer underneath the snowpack. Keep an eye out for cracks shooting across the surface or small slabs shearing off. These are signs of a potential avalanche.

WHAT TO DO IN AN AVALANCHE

SURVIVAL STATS

It is rare to survive an avalanche. 92 percent of victims survive if rescued within 18 minutes. 30 percent survive if found within 35 minutes. After one hour, only one in three survive and after two hours, the survival rate is nearly zero.

Firstly, try to get off the slab. Head straight downhill as fast as you can and then veer to the side to get out of the way. If you can't get off the slab, reach for a tree.

If you can't find a tree, ditch your skis, roll onto your back with your feet facing downhill, and swim backstroke uphill as hard as you can! This will help you stay close to the surface.

Once the avalanche stops, it will settle like concrete, making it impossible to move. As soon as it stops, put one arm across your face and punch up with the other. If you're near the surface you might break through, and if not, it will give you a bigger air pocket. Stay still to conserve oxygen.

If you see someone else swept away in an avalanche, try to work out where in the snow they are. Skis and gloves might give you a clue. Don't waste time going to find help – just start digging! As soon as you reach the victim, clear their airways.

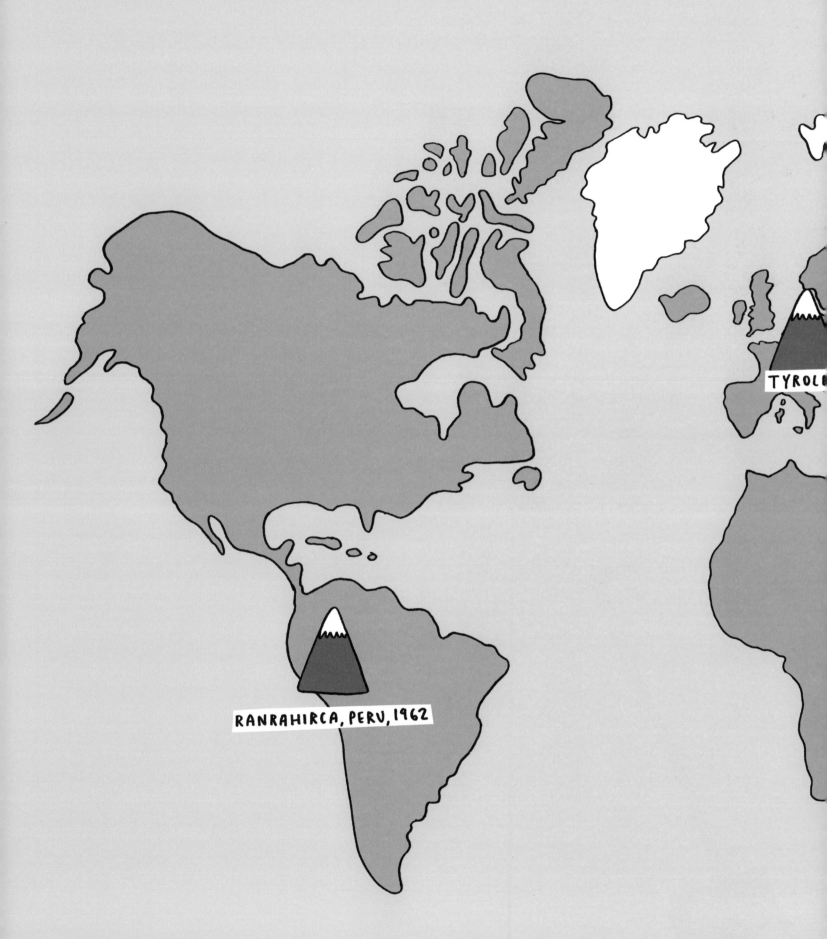

RANRAHIRCA, PERU, 1962

TYROLE

LONS, AUSTRIA, 1954

NORTH OSSETIA, RUSSIA, 2002

1916   PANJSHIR PROVINCE, AFGHANISTAN, 2015

Tyrolean Alps / 13th December 1916

In the First World War, avalanches in the Austrian-Italian Alps were triggered intentionally by firing into slopes of unstable snow. More than 10,000 troops were killed in a single day, which became known as White Friday.

Blons, Austria / 12th January 1954

A dry snow avalanche hit the village centre of Blons. Nine hours later, a second avalanche struck, wiping out the village completely and killing 200 people.

Ranrahirca, Peru / 10th January 1962

A huge slab broke loose from Mount Huascaran, and wiped out the villages of Ranrahirca and Yungai. 4,000 people were killed, making it the worst snow disaster in peacetime.

North Ossetia, Russia / 21st September 2002

When a chunk of glacier on Mount Kazbek collapsed, it triggered a 20 million ton avalanche that buried several villages, killing 150 people.

Panjshir Province, Afghanistan / 24th February 2015

A total of 40 avalanches killed 316 people when a series of snowstorms hit, destroying villages with poorly constructed houses.

What is weather? What makes it hot or cold, or rainy or cloudy? Weather happens in a layer of gasses called the atmosphere. The atmosphere is like blanket wrapped around the planet, preventing it from getting too hot or too cold. The bottom layer of the atmosphere is called the troposphere. It contains 80 percent of the atmosphere's gases and 99 percent of its water. This is where most of the world's weather occurs.

Weather is driven by differences in air pressure, temperature and moisture levels between one place and another. The people who study weather are called meteorologists. Meteorologists use tools including thermometers, anemometers, barometers and information from satellites to interpret the weather and issue warnings when a big storm is approaching.

ATMOSPHERE

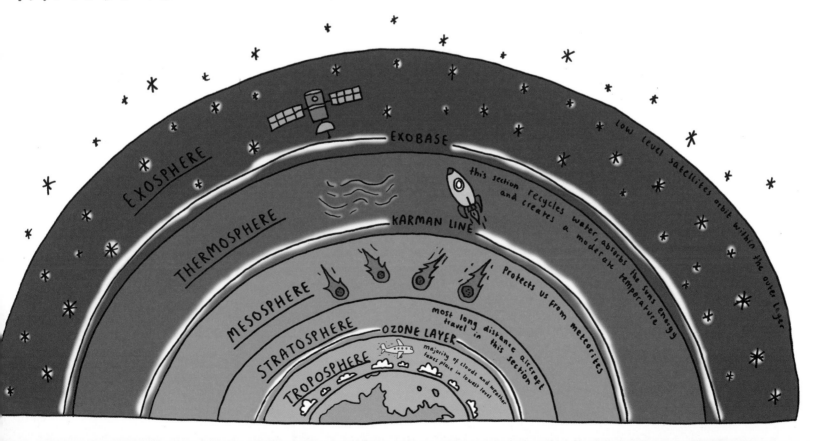

TROPICAL CYCLONES

A tropical cyclone is a rotating storm, with thunderstorms spiralling out of a low-pressure centre called the 'eye'. In the North Atlantic and Northeast Pacific, it is known as a hurricane.

A tropical cyclone has various names around the world. It is known as a typhoon in Southeast Asia, and a cyclone in the Indian Ocean.

The word 'hurricane' comes from the name of the Caribbean god of evil, Hurrican.

A tropical cyclone forms over warm tropical or sub-tropical waters. When it hits land, it brings powerful rains and winds so strong they can rip out trees and destroy buildings.

HOW DO TROPICAL CYCLONES FORM?

Tropical cyclones form when air, heated by warm ocean water (27 °C or more), starts quickly rising. As the air cools down, it is pushed aside by more warm air rising below it, creating an area of low pressure near the surface of the ocean. The 'Coriolis effect', made by the Earth's rotation, causes the winds to start spinning.

As the storm moves across the ocean, it is fed by the warm water, growing in force, and developing into a huge system of spinning clouds and wind, with an area of low pressure at its centre.

When the winds reach 120 km/h, the storm is considered tropical cyclone. A tropical cyclone can grow to 2000 km wide with clouds towering 15 km high.

As the storm moves inland, it no longer has the warm water fuelling it, and eventually loses power.

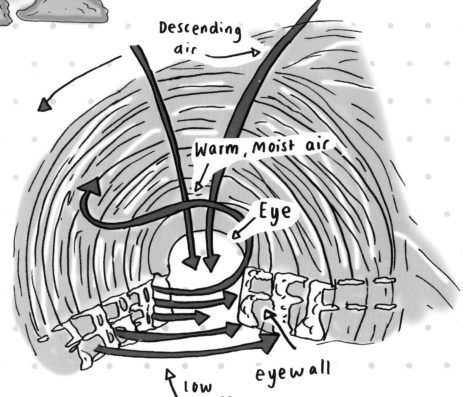

Descending air

Warm, Moist air

Eye

eyewall

low pressure

ANATOMY OF A TROPICAL CYCLONE

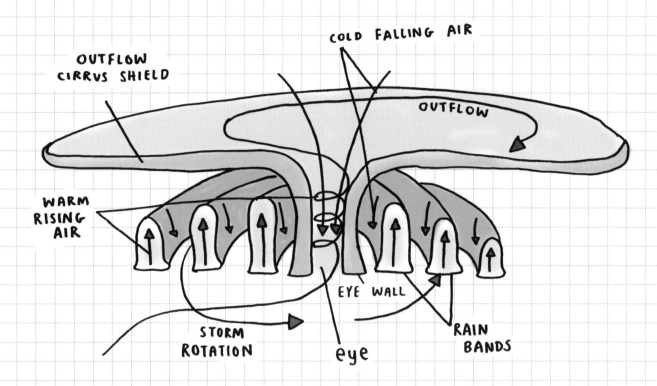

OUTFLOW CIRRUS SHIELD

COLD FALLING AIR

OUTFLOW

WARM RISING AIR

EYE WALL

STORM ROTATION

eye

RAIN BANDS

ANATOMY OF A TROPICAL CYCLONE:

THE EYE is the area of low pressure at the centre of the storm. When the eye passes overhead, the heavy rains suddenly stop and the wind is calm. But don't let this fool you – on the other side of the eye is the eye wall.

THE EYE WALL, at 15-30 km from the centre of the storm, is the most ferocious part of the hurricane. Winds at the eye wall can reach speeds of 320 km/h.

RAINBANDS are dense clouds spiralling outwards from the eye wall, with the winds weakening towards the outer region.

A big hurricane can release wind and heat energy equal to 70 times the annual world energy consumption, or the energy of 10,000 nuclear bombs!

WHEN AND WHERE?

Tropical cyclones happen all around the world in areas with warm ocean waters. They are very common in areas of the Western Pacific. Some years, the Philippines are hit by more than 20 typhoons.

In the Northern Hemisphere, the peak hurricane season is late summer/early autumn, when the difference between sea temperature and air temperature is greatest.

Although they can be devastating, tropical cyclones play an important part in regulating global temperatures, as they carry heat and energy away from the tropics and take it to milder regions.

EFFECTS OF TROPICAL CYCLONES

RAIN
Tropical cyclones can dump over 50 cm of rain in a 24-hour period, and massive flooding can occur as far as 40 km inland.

DISEASE
The standing water left after a big flood can lead to diseases like cholera and mosquito-born diseases like malaria.

STORM SURGE
The storm can make water levels rise by several meters, causing massive waves to hit the shore. This is called storm surge. It is especially dangerous when it hits during high tide, and can destroy coastal areas.

WIND
Winds are at such high speeds that they can rip up trees, blow away small buildings and damage roads, buildings and infrastructure.

TORNADOES
Small tornadoes can develop inside the eye wall of a hurricane. Sometimes it's hard to tell what damage is caused by the hurricane and what is caused by tornadoes.

MEASURING A CYCLONE

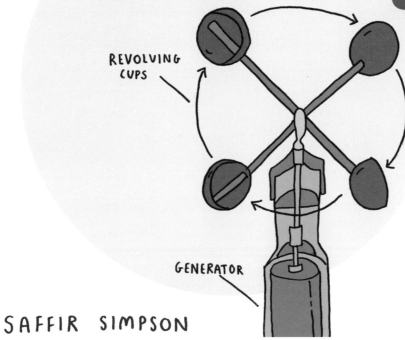

An anemometer is used to measure wind speed.

REVOLVING CUPS

GENERATOR

Tropical storms in the Atlantic alternate between boy and girl names. The first storm of the year will always start with the letter 'A', the next 'B' and so on. The names can be repeated every six years.

SAFFIR SIMPSON

Tropical Cyclones are rated on a scale from 1 (weakest) to 5 (fiercest)

	CATEGORY 1	CATEGORY 2	CATEGORY 3	CATEGORY 4	CATEGORY 5
WIND	119 - 153 kmh	154 - 177 kmh	178 - 209 kmh	210 - 249 kmh	OVER 250 kmh
STORM SURGE	4 - 5 ft	6 - 8 ft	9 - 12 ft	13 - 16 ft	over 18 ft
DAMAGE					

Although only around 20 percent of tropical cyclones fall into category 3 or above, they account for around 85 percent of the damage caused.

WARNING!
Don't use electrical appliances as lightning can cause power surges. If there is a flood, switch off your electricity.

WHAT TO DO IN A HURRICANE

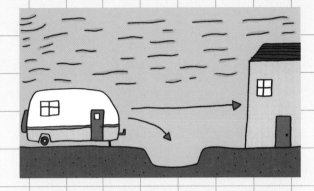

If your home isn't on higher ground or if you are in a caravan or mobile home, go to a shelter.

Stay inside – preferably in a basement, away from windows that might shatter. Don't go outside, even if it looks like the weather is clearing. It could just be the eye of the hurricane, with more storms to come.

If you are out in a car, do not try to drive through flood waters. Turn around and go back the way you came.

HURRICANE KATRINA, 2005

HURRICANE MITCH, 1998

HURRICANE MARIA, 2017

Bhola Cyclone / 1970

The deadliest cyclone ever recorded hit Bangladesh with winds of 190 km/h, killing over 300,000 people in a storm surge, which wiped out islands and villages near the Bay of Bengal.

Typhoon Nina / 1975

This typhoon hit the coast of Taiwan, causing the collapse of two big dams, which then caused another 65 dams to collapse. At least 200,000 people were killed in the resulting floods.

Hurricane Mitch / 1998

A huge, slow-moving hurricane that made landfall in Honduras and then swept across Central America. It dumped almost 2 m of rain, causing floods and landslides, killing around 11,000 people.

Hurricane Katrina / 2005

When Hurricane Katrina made landfall in Louisiana, USA, it caused the flood barriers (levees) around New Orleans to fail, flooding 80 percent of the city. Many thousands of people were stranded and around 1,600 people died.

Hurricane Maria / 2017

This category 5 hurricane hit the islands of Puerto Rico, Dominica, Martinique and Guadeloupe. Houses and roads were swept away and a slow humanitarian response meant that around 2,900 people were killed.

Cyclone Nargis / 2008

One of the deadliest cyclones to hit Asia, Nargis made landfall in Myanmar, sending a storm surge that caused extreme flooding in densely populated areas. The official death toll was around 140,000, but the real number could be up to 1 million.

BHOLA CYCLONE, 1970

CYCLONE NARGIS, 2008

TYPHOON NINA, 1975

TORNADOES

A tornado is a spinning funnel of air that is in contact with the Earth below and a cumulonimbus cloud above. The winds of a tornado are the strongest on the planet, reaching up to 500 km/h.

The extremely high winds of a tornado can destroy buildings, uproot trees, suck the water from a riverbed and send cars flying through the air. They can injure or kill people by dragging them along the ground or dropping them from dangerous heights. Flying debris is also a major cause of injury.

An average tornado is 200 m wide and travels a distance of 10 km, leaving a long, narrow path of destruction in its wake. It can destroy a house but leave the one next door completely intact.

Tornadoes can happen anywhere in the world. There are a lot of tornadoes in the United Kingdom and the Netherlands. However, 75 percent of all tornadoes happen in the United States in an area of the Great Plains known as Tornado Alley. The conditions there are perfect for tornadoes, as the dry, cold air from Canada meets the warm, moist air travelling up from the Gulf of Mexico.

SUPERCELL TORNADOES

90 percent of tornadoes form during what is known as a supercell storm, or rotating thunderstorm. This is a thunderstorm with rising, spiral air currents called rotating updrafts. A tornado forms when warm, moist air near the ground rises to meet colder, dry air above the storm. The rotating updraft swirls the air together, forming a tube of air.

The tube starts off horizontally, but as more warm air rises, it grows, spinning faster and faster and tilting vertically down towards the area of low pressure where the air has been rising. As it gets longer, it becomes a funnel cloud. When the funnel touches the ground, it becomes a tornado.

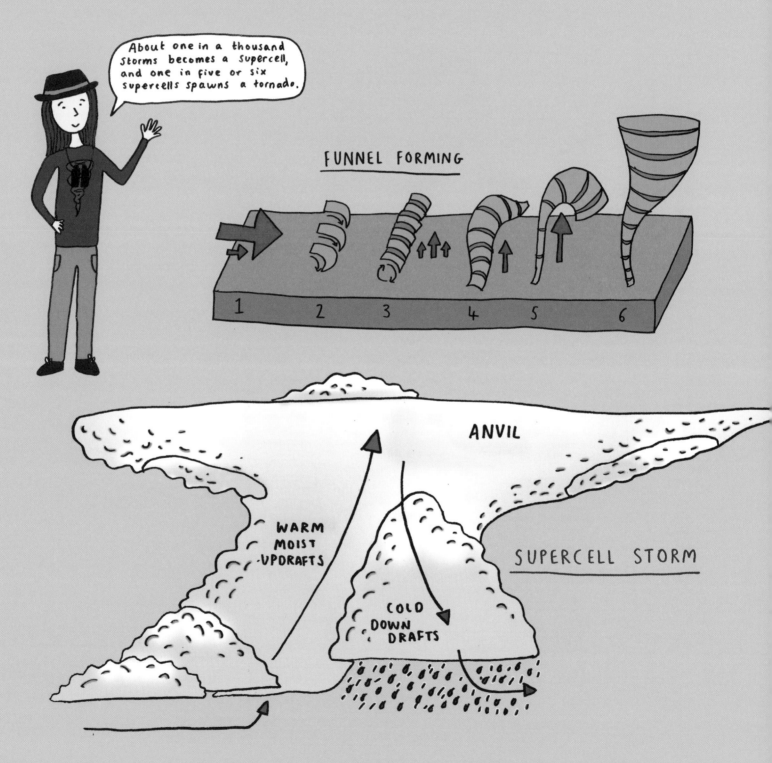

About one in a thousand storms becomes a supercell, and one in five or six supercells spawns a tornado.

FUNNEL FORMING

1   2   3   4   5   6

ANVIL

WARM MOIST UPDRAFTS

COLD DOWN DRAFTS

SUPERCELL STORM

LANDSPOUT TORNADOES

Also known as a 'dust tube' tornado, a landspout tornado forms when vertically spinning air near the ground is stretched up to a cloud by an updraft. In other words, it happens from the ground up, rather than the cloud down. It has a narrow, rope-like funnel that is surrounded by a fluffy dust-haze. Landspouts can cause damage, but they are much weaker than supercell tornadoes, lasting 15 minutes or less and usually rating no more than EF2 (see p. 66).

A waterspout is a similar phenomenon that occurs over water.

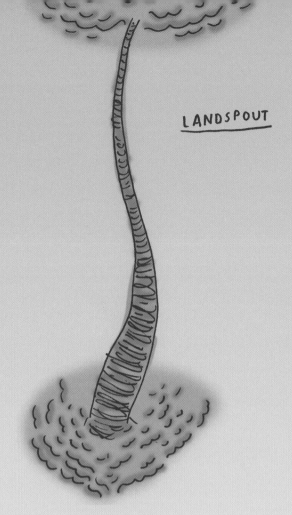

LANDSPOUT

ANATOMY OF A TORNADO

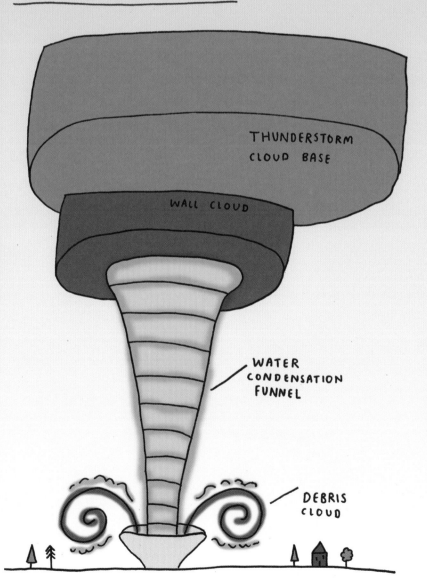

THUNDERSTORM CLOUD BASE

WALL CLOUD

WATER CONDENSATION FUNNEL

DEBRIS CLOUD

Sometimes the sky turns a greeny-yellow colour before a tornado. Scientists do not know why this is. Some think that the golden light from a low sun combines with the blue sky through the filter of the thunderclouds to create a greenish tinge.

ANATOMY OF A TORNADO

Underneath the thundercloud, a thick pedestal cloud forms, called a 'rotating wall cloud'. This is where the strongest updrafts concentrate. The condensation funnel is made of water droplets. It stretches from the wall cloud to the ground. At the base of the funnel there is often a cloud of debris, which can hide the funnel completely, making it difficult to detect.

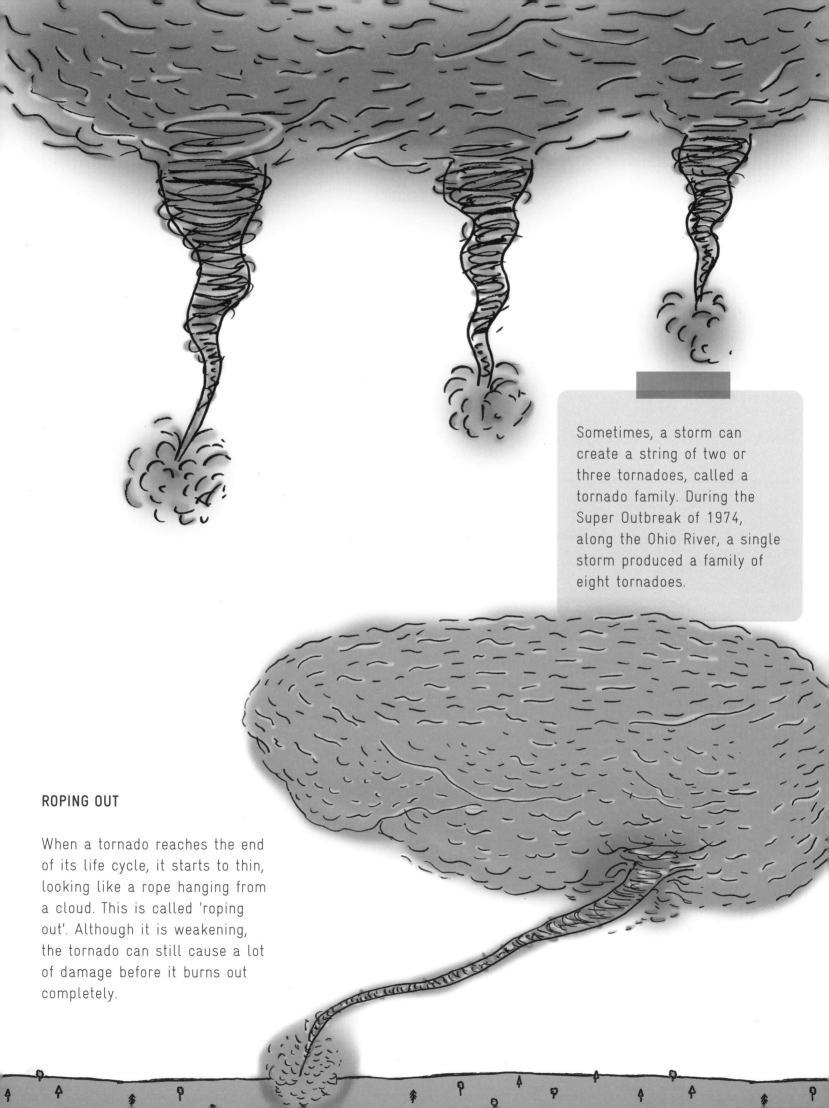

Sometimes, a storm can create a string of two or three tornadoes, called a tornado family. During the Super Outbreak of 1974, along the Ohio River, a single storm produced a family of eight tornadoes.

ROPING OUT

When a tornado reaches the end of its life cycle, it starts to thin, looking like a rope hanging from a cloud. This is called 'roping out'. Although it is weakening, the tornado can still cause a lot of damage before it burns out completely.

SHAPES

We are used to seeing rope or cone shaped tornadoes, but tornadoes come in all different shapes and sizes. An average tornado measures around 150 m across, whilst a huge wedge tornado can measure two kilometres across or more.

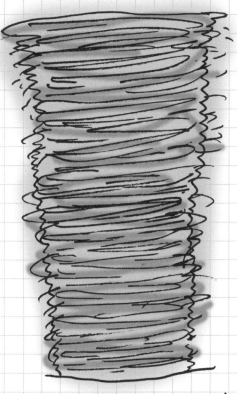

long and cylindrical.

WEDGE TORNADO

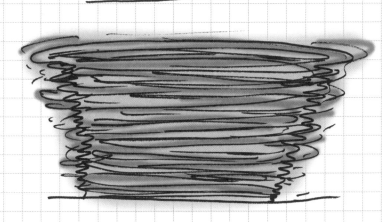

At least as wide as they are high. Usually very big and destructive.

MULTIPLE VORTEX TORNADO

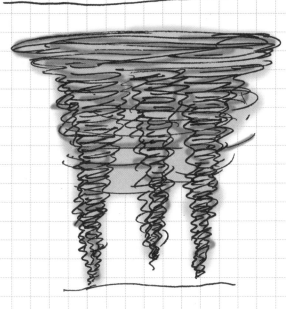

contains small individual tornadoes rotating around a common centre.

CONE TORNADO

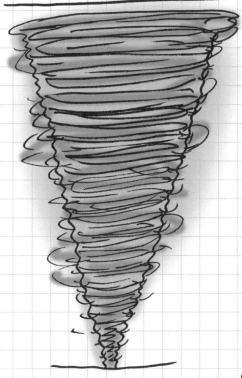

A funnel that is narrow at the bottom, widening up towards the top.

63

DETECTING A TORNADO

In 1953, meteorologists discovered that radars picked up a certain shape when a storm was about to form a tornado. This shape, called a 'hook echo', allowed them to detect a tornado-producing storm.

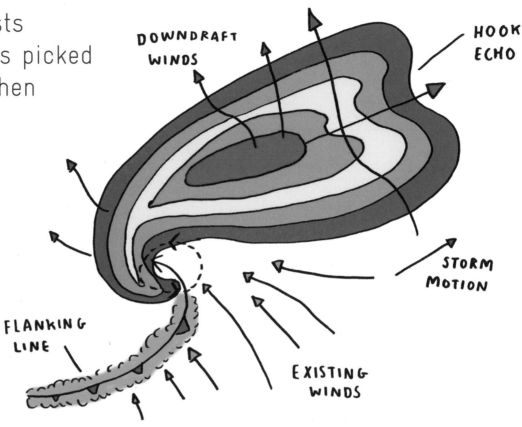

DOWNDRAFT WINDS

HOOK ECHO

STORM MOTION

FLANKING LINE

EXISTING WINDS

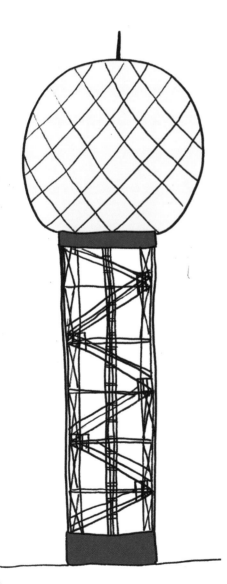

Today, radars measure the speed and direction of the winds of a storm, detecting a supercell storm that could be brewing 160 km away.

However, these radars only detect potential tornadoes, not actual tornadoes, and so in the USA, meteorologists rely on trained 'storm spotters' to identify and report on tornadoes as they form. Storm spotters will be looking to see if a storm has the characteristics of a supercell storm: a dome-like top that reaches up into the stratosphere, a corkscrew movement and rotating wall clouds. They will then watch the storm, reporting real time warnings.

SKYWARN

THE STORM SPOTTING PROGRAMME IN THE USA IS CALLED SKYWARN.

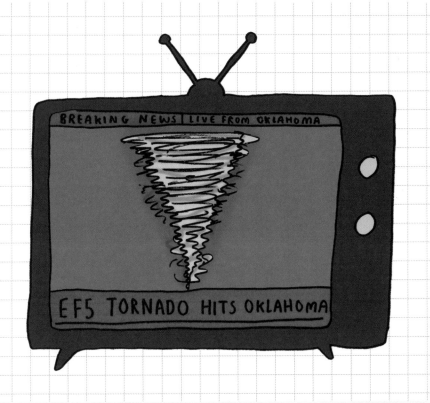

BREAKING NEWS | LIVE FROM OKLAHOMA

EF5 TORNADO HITS OKLAHOMA

An average tornado lasts around eight minutes and travels between five and ten kilometres at speeds of 45 km/h, usually moving in an easterly or north-easterly direction.

However, occasionally, a huge wedge tornado can reach up to four kilometres across, last up to three hours, and travel at speeds of 480 km/h! These are called 'long track' tornadoes.

There is an average of 1,200 tornadoes in the USA every year, but most of those are quite small. Big tornadoes only account for two percent, but cause 80 percent of damage and fatalities. Tornadoes kill an average of 70 people and cause about 400 million dollars worth of damage in the USA every year.

Texas reports the most tornadoes of any other state.

Tornado wind and debris cause most of the structural damage suffered, but nearly half of all injuries happen after the tornado, during rescue work and clean-up. According to the Federal Emergency Management Agency, a third of these injuries come from stepping on nails!

MEASURING A TORNADO

Because the wind from a tornado is so strong, normal wind speed measuring devices would be instantly destroyed. Meteorologists therefore use the Enhanced Fujita (EF) Scale to measure the intensity of a tornado. The EF Scale measures the damage caused by a tornado to estimate its windpower.

EF#	WIND SPEED (kmh)		DAMAGES
0	105-137		**Light damage:** Branches broken off trees, gutters broken, tiles blown off roofs.
1	138-177		**Moderate damage:** Roofs damaged, caravans overturned, windows broken, doors blown off.
2	179-217		**Considerable damage:** Roofs blown off, trees snapped, cars lifted off the ground.
3	219-266		**Severe damage:** Houses destroyed, large buildings damaged, trains overturned.
4	267-322		**Devastating damage:** Houses levelled, cars and trucks thrown large distances.
5	322+		**Incredible damage:** Houses and tall buildings are torn apart so quickly they seem to 'explode'. Roads are peeled up, riverbeds sucked dry and towns reduced to rubble.

LISTENING FOR A TORNADO

Tornadoes are usually preceded by thunderstorms or hailstorms. However, they can also occur when it is not raining. In fact, in the Great Plains it very rarely rains during a tornado. If you hear a loud rumble, be on alert. Tornadoes are very loud and as they get nearer they can sound like the roar of a jet engine.

WHAT TO DO IN A TORNADO

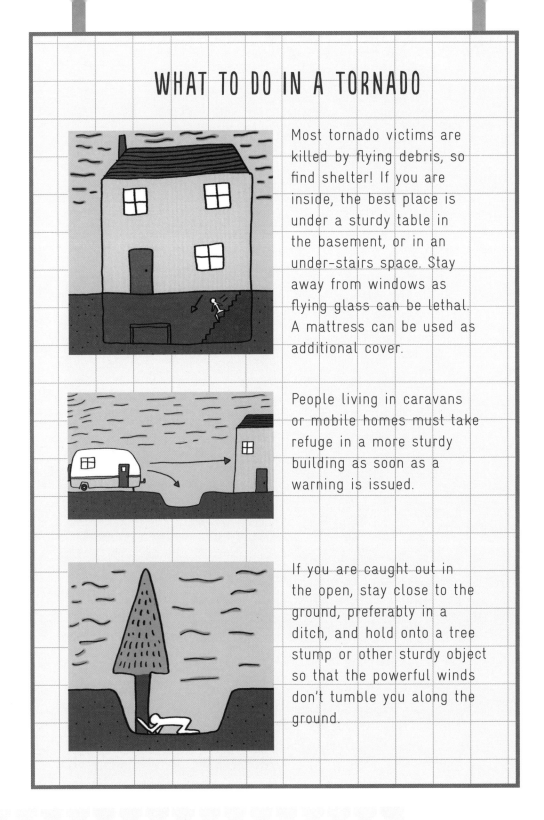

Most tornado victims are killed by flying debris, so find shelter! If you are inside, the best place is under a sturdy table in the basement, or in an under-stairs space. Stay away from windows as flying glass can be lethal. A mattress can be used as additional cover.

People living in caravans or mobile homes must take refuge in a more sturdy building as soon as a warning is issued.

If you are caught out in the open, stay close to the ground, preferably in a ditch, and hold onto a tree stump or other sturdy object so that the powerful winds don't tumble you along the ground.

TALL TORNADO TALES

There is a myth that closed windows can cause a building to explode, due to the difference in air pressure. But in fact, buildings 'explode' simply because of the force of wind.

Another myth is that if you spot a tornado, you should drive away at a right angle. However, tornadoes do not always travel in a straight line. It is much wiser to leave the car and take shelter in a nearby building.

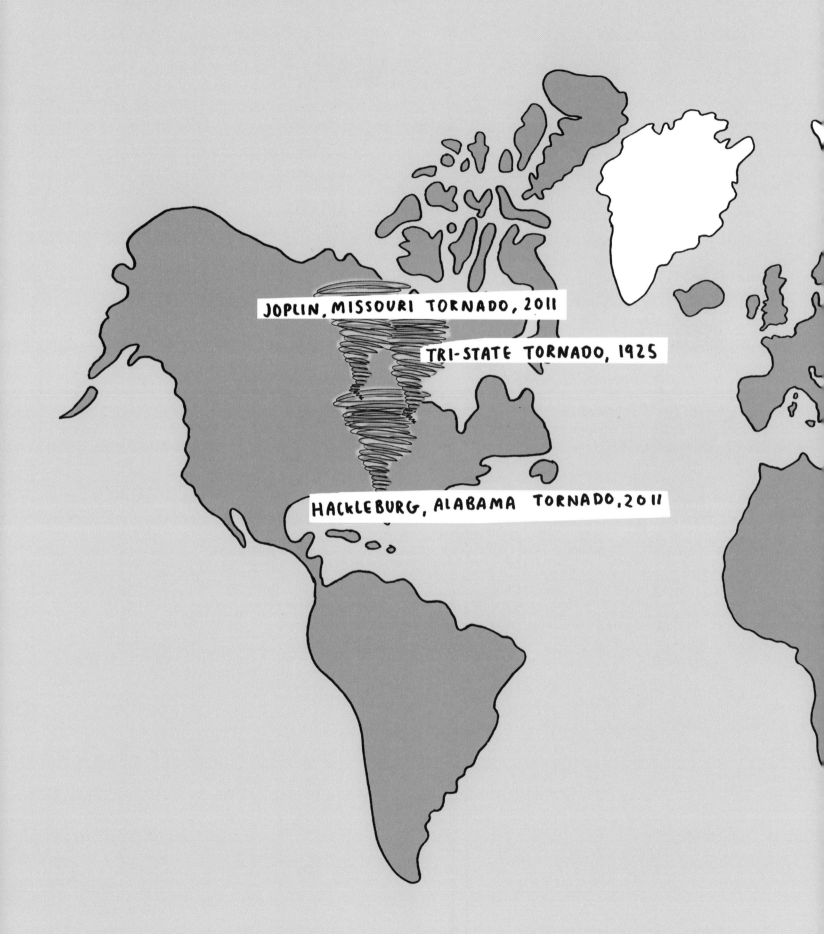

JOPLIN, MISSOURI TORNADO, 2011

TRI-STATE TORNADO, 1925

HACKLEBURG, ALABAMA TORNADO, 2011

IVANOVO TORNADOES, 1984

DAULATPUR-SATURIA TORNADO, BANGLADESH, 1989

Daulatpur-Saturia Tornado, Bangladesh / 26th April 1989

This 1 km wide tornado swept through a poverty stricken area. Poor construction meant that 1,300 people were killed and 80,000 left homeless.

Tri-State Tornado, USA / 18th March, 1925

The deadliest tornado in US history. With winds of 480 km/h, it cleared a 320 km path through Missouri, Indiana and Illinois, causing a death toll of 695 and destroying 15,000 homes.

Joplin, Missouri Tornado, USA / 22nd May 2011

With winds of over 300 km/h, this tornado injured thousands and killed 158 people.

Hackleburg, Alabama Tornado / Apr 27th 2011

Part of the 2011 'superoutbreak' of tornadoes, this storm tossed vehicles to distances of 150 m as it went on its 200 km rampage.

Ivanovo Tornado Outbreak, Russia / 9th June 1984

This was a very rare event for the area. A family of tornadoes hit an area north of Moscow, with at least of two of them registering EF5. They wiped large buildings off the ground, killing at least 92 people.

BLIZZARDS

A blizzard is an intense snowstorm with very low temperatures, strong winds of over 56 km/h and very low visibility for a period of three hours or more.

The difference between the common snowstorm, and the less common blizzard, is not snowfall but strength of wind, which is much more fierce in a blizzard. Some blizzards don't have any falling snow – the winds blow the ground snow up, limiting visibility. This is called a ground blizzard.

Extreme blizzards have wind-speeds of over 72 km/h, and temperatures of -12 °C or lower. They can cause complete whiteout, meaning that it is impossible to see even as far as your hands.

WINTER PRECIPITATION CHART

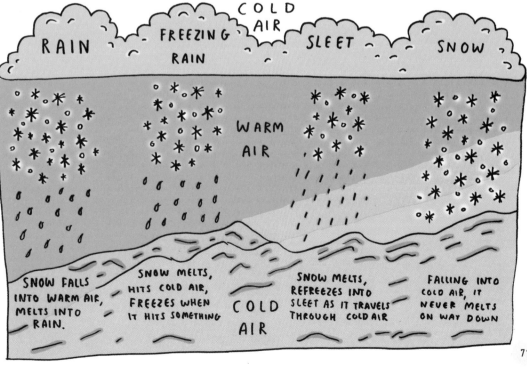

RAIN · FREEZING RAIN · COLD AIR · SLEET · SNOW

WARM AIR

COLD AIR

SNOW FALLS INTO WARM AIR, MELTS INTO RAIN.

SNOW MELTS, HITS COLD AIR, FREEZES WHEN IT HITS SOMETHING

SNOW MELTS, REFREEZES INTO SLEET AS IT TRAVELS THROUGH COLD AIR

FALLING INTO COLD AIR, IT NEVER MELTS ON WAY DOWN

WHAT TO DO IN A BLIZZARD

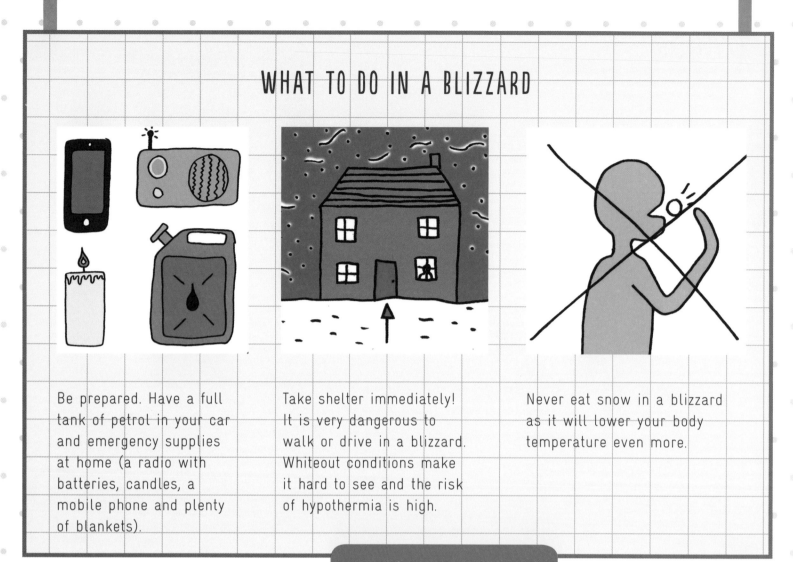

Be prepared. Have a full tank of petrol in your car and emergency supplies at home (a radio with batteries, candles, a mobile phone and plenty of blankets).

Take shelter immediately! It is very dangerous to walk or drive in a blizzard. Whiteout conditions make it hard to see and the risk of hypothermia is high.

Never eat snow in a blizzard as it will lower your body temperature even more.

EFFECTS OF A BLIZZARD

Blizzards can be extremely dangerous. People trapped outside in a blizzard will quickly suffer hypothermia, frostbite and nerve damage.

Blizzards can damage communications and power lines, often leaving towns stranded in unreachable conditions for days at a time. Roof cave-ins and uprooted trees are common. Flooding often happens after a blizzard, when snow melts faster than the ground can absorb it.

We might imagine blizzards in the mountains, but it's usually snowstorms that hit mountain areas. The flat terrain of plains provides the perfect conditions for winds to reach blizzard speed.

The term 'blizzard' originally meant a volley of musket fire. It was first used to describe a snowstorm in Iowa in the 1870s.

HAILSTORMS

A hailstorm is a weather phenomenon in which balls of ice, called hailstones, fall from the sky. Most hailstones are around half a centimetre in diameter, but they can grow to the size of grapefruits. When balls of ice this size fall from the sky at speeds of up to 170 km/h, they can cause a lot of damage.

The largest hailstone ever recorded was in South Dakota in 2010. It measured 20 cm in diameter and weighed almost a kilogram!

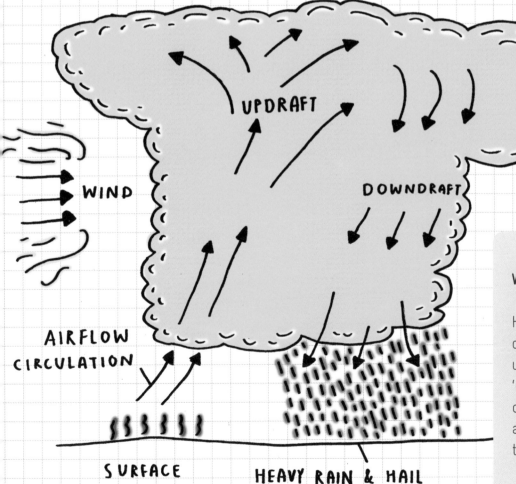

ANVIL

UPDRAFT

WIND

DOWNDRAFT

AIRFLOW CIRCULATION

SURFACE HEATING

HEAVY RAIN & HAIL

WHERE DOES HAIL FORM?

Hail forms in large, anvil-shaped cumulonimbus clouds with upward moving air currents called 'updrafts'. Cumulonimbus clouds can reach 20,000 km up into the atmosphere. The temperature at the top of the clouds can reach -20 °C.

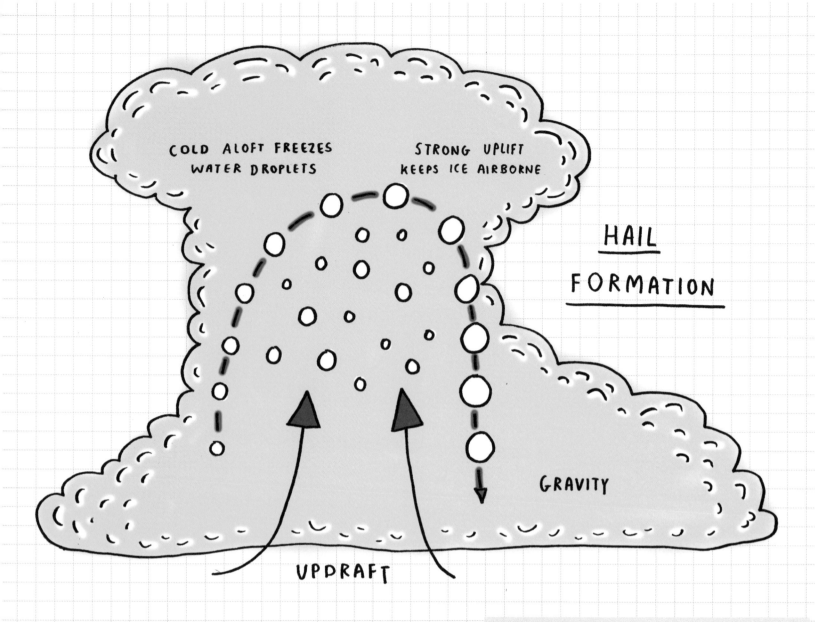

COLD ALOFT FREEZES WATER DROPLETS

STRONG UPLIFT KEEPS ICE AIRBORNE

HAIL
FORMATION

GRAVITY

UPDRAFT

HOW DOES HAIL FORM?

Hailstones start as frozen water droplets called 'hail embryos'. The updrafts bounce these hail embryos around the cloud where they meet with other supercooled droplets of water and start to grow. When they reach the bottom of the cloud, they become coated in a layer of moisture, and when they bounce up to the top again, this layer freezes, so that the hail embryo grows, layer by layer, like an onion. When it gets too heavy, it falls to the ground as a hailstone.

DID YOU KNOW: If you slice a large hailstone in half, you can see rings of ice. Clear layers form in the top of the cloud and milky layers form lower down. If you count the rings you can tell how many times the hailstone bounced to the bottom of the cloud and back up again!

HAILSTONE SHAPES AND SIZES

Usually, when a hailstone reaches 0.5 mm, gravity pulls it to earth. But in a stormcloud with strong updrafts, the hailstone can keep growing in the upper part of the cloud, only falling to earth when it is really huge.

Sometimes hailstones stick to each other as they bounce around. This is called aggregation hail, and these hailstones look spiky and asymmetrical.

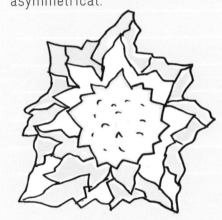

HAILSTONE DAMAGE		
SIZE	HAIL SIZE	DAMAGE
one pound (£1)	2.5 cm	DAMAGE TO SHINGLES
Golf ball	4.5 cm	DENTS ON CARS
orange	7 cm	WINDSHIELDS SMASHED
Grapefruit	11.5 cm	HOLES IN HOUSE AND CAR ROOFS

EFFECTS OF HAILSTORMS

Hail does a lot of damage to crops and agriculture. Even small hail can flatten a field of wheat in minutes. Soy and corn are very vulnerable crops.

When a storm produces hailstones larger than 2 cm in diameter it is considered severe. A severe hailstorm can cause a lot of damage to property; denting cars, smashing windscreens and even puncturing holes in roofs.

It is rare for hail to cause death, as there is usually enough time to find shelter, but on occasion it has been known to cause fatal head injuries.

WHAT TO DO IN A HAILSTORM

If you are inside, move away from the windows in case they shatter.

If you are outside, seek shelter immediately – ideally in a building, but if not, then in a car. Don't shelter under trees, as they may be struck by lightning.

If there is really no shelter, protect your head however you can. Your shoes will give some protection in a worst-case scenario.

If you are driving, pull over. Wrap your head in a coat and turn to face the centre of the car to protect yourself from broken glass.

Some parts of the world experience a lot of hail. The monsoon season in India brings thunderstorms and hail. Australia and China also experience frequent hailstorms. The Great Plains region in the Midwestern USA experiences a hailstorm season that lasts from March to October.

It may be surprising to know that a lot of hailstorms happen in summer. This is because big clouds are more likely to develop at warmer times of the year. The hail that falls during the summer months will quickly melt, bringing a danger of flash flooding.

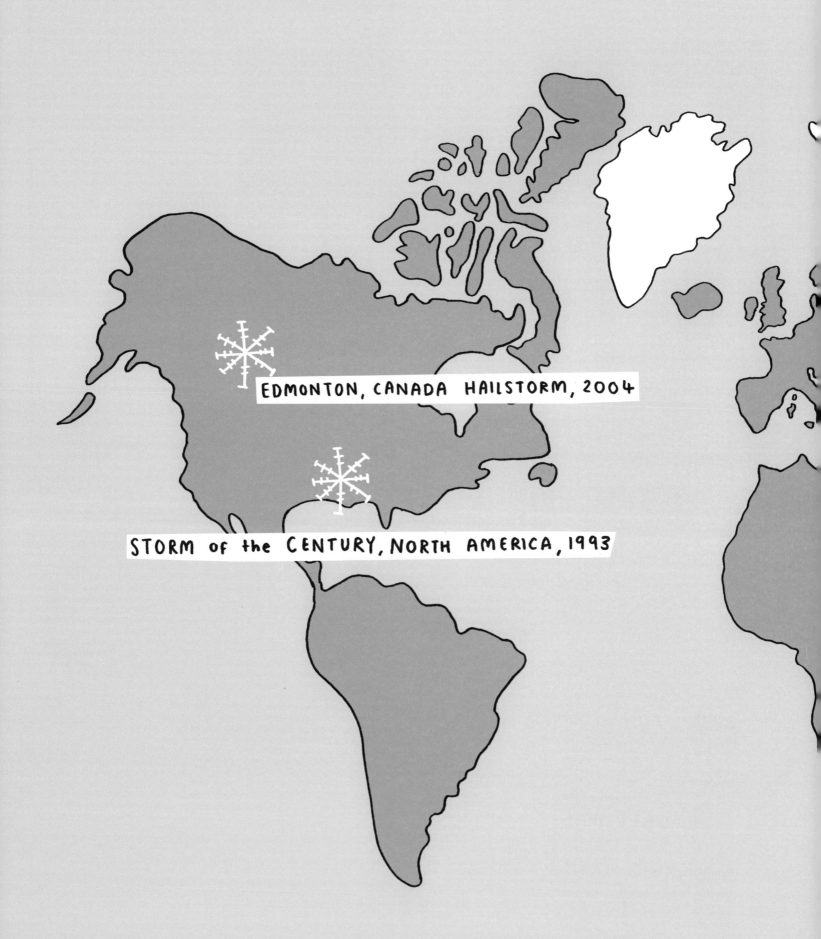

EDMONTON, CANADA HAILSTORM, 2004

STORM of the CENTURY, NORTH AMERICA, 1993

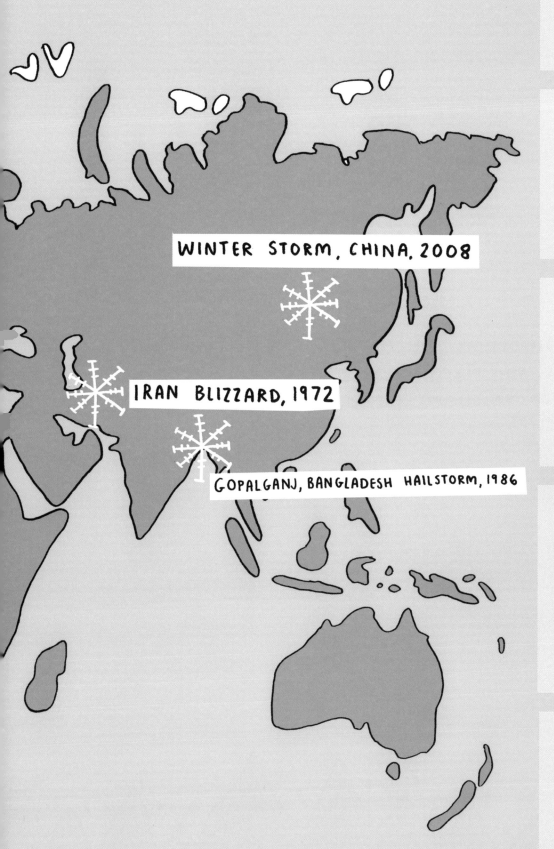

WINTER STORM, CHINA, 2008

IRAN BLIZZARD, 1972

GOPALGANJ, BANGLADESH HAILSTORM, 1986

Gopalganj, Bangladesh Hailstorm / 1986

A vicious hailstorm in the area of a refugee camp killed a total of 92 people and caused a ferry to capsize. The heaviest hailstone on record, weighing 1 kg, was found in this storm.

Edmonton, Canada Hailstorm / 2004

A 30 minute storm produced hailstones the size of golf balls and left a blanket of ice 6 cm deep on the ground. The weight of the hail caused the glass roof of a shopping centre to shatter.

Iran Blizzard / 1972

The deadliest blizzard in history dumped more than 5 m of snow on top of villages around Ardakan in southern Iran, burying them completely and resulting in the deaths of around 4,000 people.

Storm of the Century, North America / 1993

Also known as 'The Great Blizzard', this storm stretched from Canada to Honduras with record cold temperatures, loss of electrical power, and 33 cm snow dumped as far south as Alabama. A total of 208 people died in the storm.

Winter Storm, China / 2008

A series of winter storms and blizzards hit central and Southern China, causing the destruction of around 200,000 homes, and 200 deaths. It also caused the loss of many crops, which led to food shortages.

WILDFIRES

A wildfire is a large, destructive, uncontrolled fire that spreads quickly over woodland or brush. Also called a forest fire, grass fire or bush fire, these fires can burn for weeks or even months, wiping out large swathes of land and all the wildlife that inhabits it.

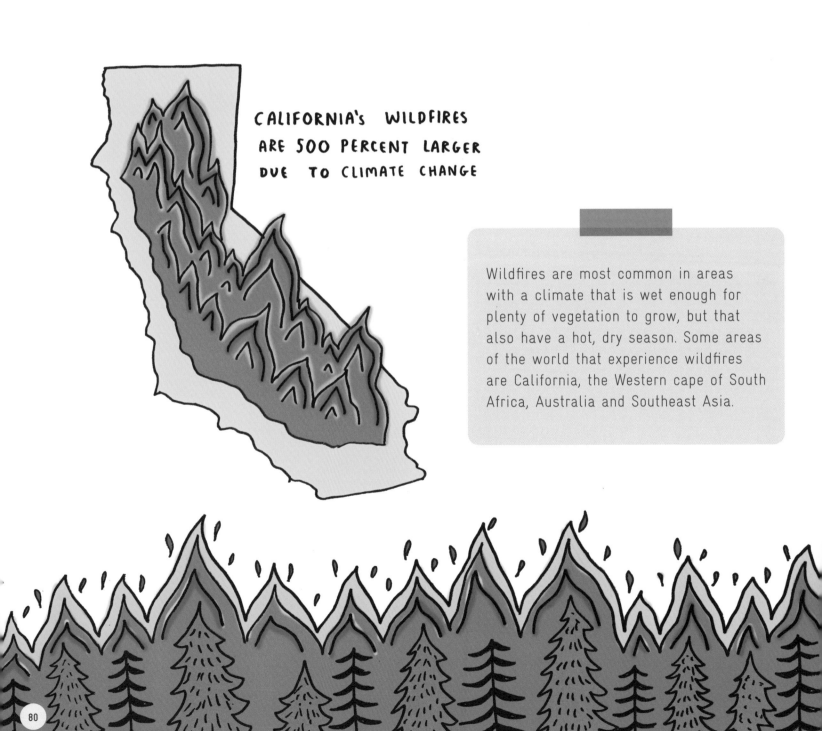

CALIFORNIA'S WILDFIRES ARE 500 PERCENT LARGER DUE TO CLIMATE CHANGE

Wildfires are most common in areas with a climate that is wet enough for plenty of vegetation to grow, but that also have a hot, dry season. Some areas of the world that experience wildfires are California, the Western cape of South Africa, Australia and Southeast Asia.

HOW DO THEY HAPPEN?

Four out of five wildfires are started by people. Campfires, discarded cigarettes, burning rubbish, fireworks and sparks from electrical equipment can all start fires. Natural causes like lightning and volcanic eruptions can also start fires, especially in very remote areas.

For any fire to ignite, there are three elements that must be present: fuel, oxygen and heat. Firefighters call this the 'fire triangle'.

- **FUEL** means the materials that feed the fire. In the case of wildfires, this is usually plant life – dry leaves, branches, grasses etc.
- **OXYGEN** in the air reacts with the energy stored inside the fuel, resulting in heat.
- **HEAT** then removes the moisture from nearby plants, making them easily flammable and continuing the cycle.

To stop the spread of a fire you have to remove one of these elements to break the triangle.

SPREADING

Once a wildfire has started, some factors can combine to cause it to spread more quickly:

TEMPERATURE

A long, hot spell will dry out plant life, making it ideal fuel for a fire. A lot of wildfires start in the afternoon, as this is often the hottest time of the day.

FIRE WHIRLS CAN HURL FLAMING LOGS OVER GREAT DISTANCES.

WIND

A hot dry wind will propel the fire forward, supplying it with more oxygen. If the wind suddenly changes direction, the fire can 'jump' into new areas, sometimes in the form of fireballs called 'firebrands'.

Really violent wildfires will generate their own winds, resulting in 'fire whirls'. These are like tornadoes that get caught in the spinning heat.

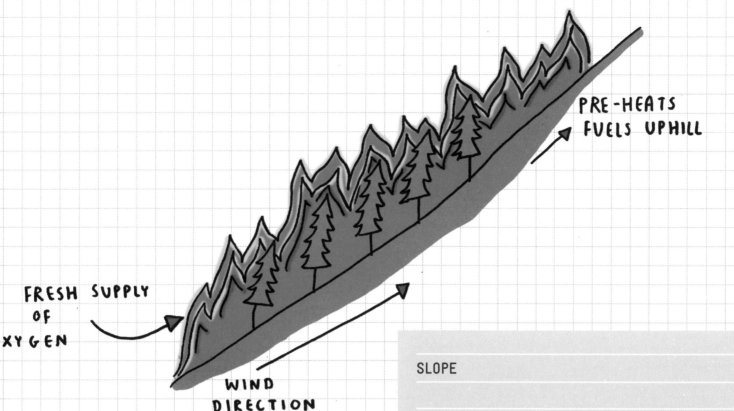

FRESH SUPPLY
OF
XYGEN

WIND
DIRECTION

PRE-HEATS
FUELS UPHILL

SLOPE

Wildfires move faster uphill, and the steeper the slope, the faster they burn. This is because wind usually flows uphill and also because heat rises, pre-heating the fuel for the fire to consume.

FUEL

The amount of flammable material in an area is called the 'fuel load'. Some types of fuel are more flammable than others. Plants and trees with a lot of moisture will slow down a fire, whilst dry grasses, dead leaves and dry brush will speed it up.

Some trees, like the eucalyptus, have evolved to survive and even encourage fires, so that they can eliminate competition from other tree species. They contain flammable oils that burn easily.

Eucalyptus leaves catch fire easily and when the fire burns through them, it moves on to the next tree, leaving the trunk intact, which will then regenerate.

TYPES OF WILDFIRE

There are three different types of wildfire. A big wildfire will combine all three types.

Ground fires feed off organic materials in the soil, like peat. This is a slow burning fire that happens underneath a layer of moist vegetation.

Surface fires burn the grasses, dry leaves, twigs and branches that are lying on the ground. These fires burn at a lower temperature than crown fires (see below) and can either spread slowly or quickly, depending on the conditions.

Crown fires burn the tops of the trees. They are the most dramatic fires, with huge flames that jump from treetop to treetop, spreading quickly if there is a hot, dry wind blowing them onwards.

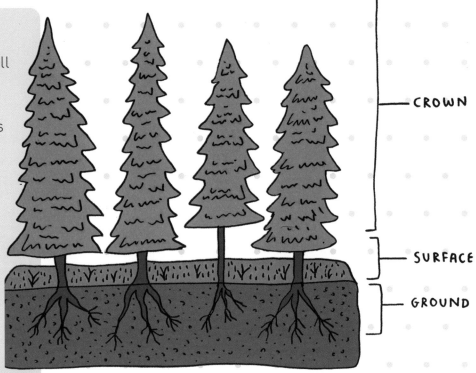

CROWN

SURFACE

GROUND

Wildfires are not necessarily bad, and can be part of a natural cycle of renewal. Some ecosystems rely on fires to burn off dead and decaying matter, making room for new plant growth. Smaller wildfires will burn away dry underbrush that could provide fuel for a bigger fire. Many plants grow back easily, and some seeds are designed to open up in the heat, finding a welcome home in the ash-enriched soil.

The problem is that with global warming, wildfires are becoming more common and more vicious. A huge, raging wildfire will scorch all nutrients out of the soil, making it harder for plants to renew their growth, and leaving slopes bare and prone to erosion. Invasive plant species can then take root, and they are often more flammable than native species, creating a likelihood of more fires.

HOW TO FIGHT FIRES

Forest fires can be enormous in size and may quickly change direction, making them extremely difficult to control. Sometimes it takes many weeks or even months to extinguish the fire completely.

These are a few methods that firefighters use to break the fire triangle:

They douse the fire with water and fire retardants using special planes called air tankers.

Using bulldozers, they clear the land in a ring around the fire to deprive it of fuel. This is called a firebreak.

Firefighters jump out of planes and put out small fires to stop them from spreading. They also set backfires. These are small, controlled fires that move in the direction of the main fire, consuming the fuel before the big fire can get there.

EFFECTS OF WILDFIRE

Once a fire begins, it can spread at a rate of 23 km/h, consuming everything in its path. Within a matter of days, it can lay waste to vast forest ecosystems, destroying all plant and animal life within. A raging wildfire will also damage villages and towns in its path.

WHAT TO DO IN A WILDFIRE

Evacuate as soon as you are told to do so.

If you are trapped indoors, fill bathtubs and sinks with water and keep windows and doors closed but unlocked.

If you are caught outside in a wildfire, keep low and hold a moist cloth over your face.

Try to find an area clear of trees and vegetation. Look for the lowest point in that area – ideally a ditch or a gully. Lie face down in it and cover your body with wet clothing or soil.

If you are in your car, don't drive around – a fire can be very disorienting.

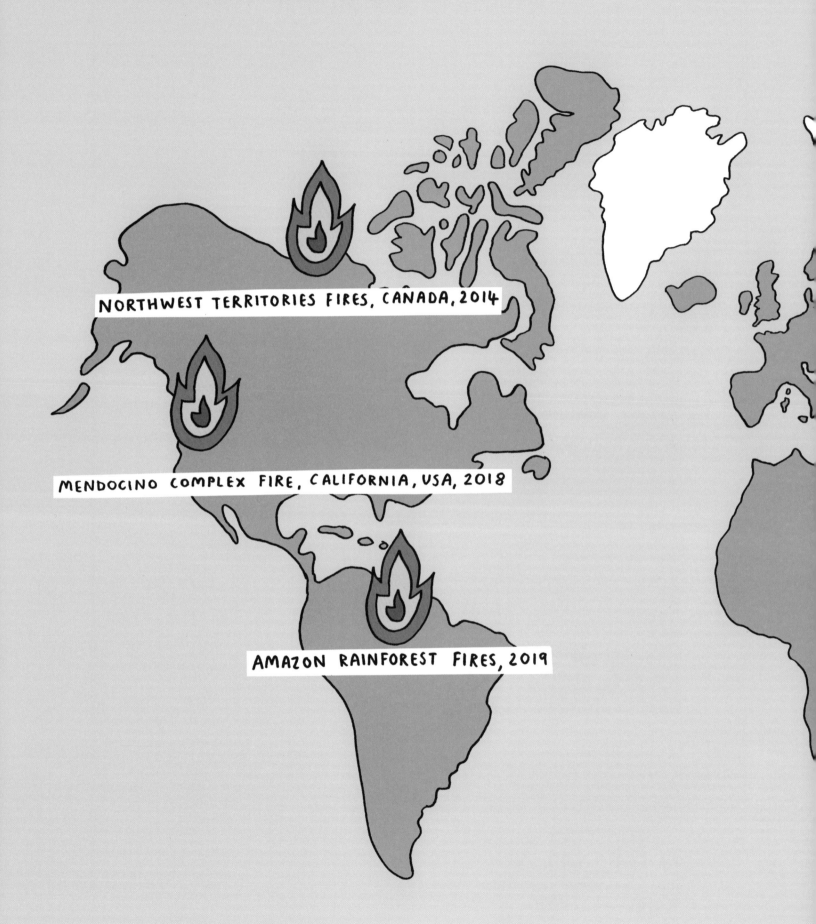

NORTHWEST TERRITORIES FIRES, CANADA, 2014

MENDOCINO COMPLEX FIRE, CALIFORNIA, USA, 2018

AMAZON RAINFOREST FIRES, 2019

Indonesian Forest Fires / 1997

Throughout the year, fires swept through the forests of Indonesia, wiping out more than 97,000 km^2 of forest, releasing 2.6 gigatonnes of CO_2 into the atmosphere and killing 240 people in the biggest fire of all time. The fire was a result of the logging of the forest to turn it into palm oil plantations as well as a big programme of swamp draining.

Black Saturday Bushfires, Australia / 2009

A series of bushfires swept through the state of Victoria following an intense heatwave. 180 people were killed, 500 injured and 2,000 homes destroyed. 4,500 km^2 of bushland was scorched.

Mendocino Complex Fire, California / 2018

Two huge wildfires spread across Northern California destroying 1,900 km^2 land, and taking two months to contain. There were no fatalities, but a lot of environmental damage was caused in the worst forest fire in California's history.

Amazon Rainforest Fires / 2019

Vast wildfires broke out across the Amazon rainforest in Brazil, Bolivia, Paraguay and Peru, with at least 20,000 km^2 of rainforest lost. It is suspected that many of the fires were set deliberately to clear land for farming.

INDONESIAN FOREST FIRES, 1997

CK SATURDAY BUSHFIRES, VICTORIA, AUSTRALIA, 2009

CLIMATE CHANGE AND NATURAL DISASTERS

TREES ABSORB CO_2, BUT MANY RAINFORESTS ARE BEING CUT DOWN TO MAKE ROOM FOR FARMLAND.

The word 'climate' refers to the weather conditions of an area over a period of 30 years.

Our planet has a clever system of balancing global climate. Surrounding the Earth is a layer of gasses called the atmosphere. The atmosphere allows some of the sun's heat to stay trapped, whilst some of it escapes. This prevents the planet getting too hot or too cold. But in the past few centuries, the planet has started warming up fast. Faster than at any other time we know about.

The reason for this is the production of gasses called greenhouse gasses. These are gasses that allow heat to come in, but don't allow it to escape, causing the Earth's temperature to rise, changing its climate. One of the main greenhouse gasses is carbon dioxide, or CO_2, which is released when we burn fossil fuels like oil and gas, which we use to power our cars and electricity plants and factories.

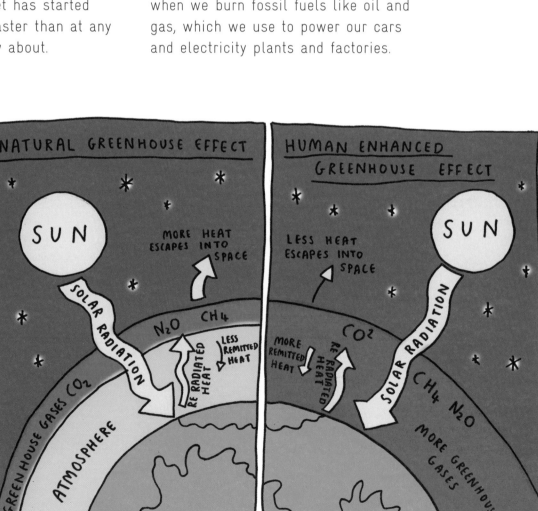

CLIMATE CHANGE AND METEOROLOGICAL DISASTERS

As the planet warms, we will see more weather extremes.

FLOODS: As polar ice caps melt, sea levels will rise, causing flooding to many coastal areas. Storm surges and high tides will become more common. As the planet heats up, more water vapour will be released into the atmosphere, allowing powerful storms to develop.

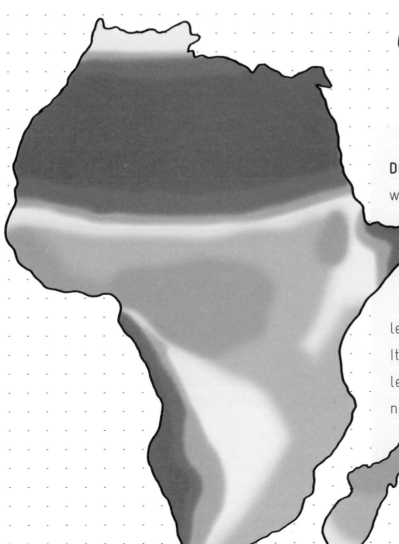

DROUGHTS: A drought is a long period of dry weather that can last months or years. During a drought, plant life dies and this quickly impacts on the wildlife that feeds on that plant life. It also affects humans, who rely on agriculture for food. When crops die, this leads to food shortages and sometimes to famine. It becomes hard to find clean drinking water, leading to disease and health crises. Areas that now experience occasional drought are likely to experience regular, long periods of drought.

BLIZZARDS, HAILSTORMS AND AVALANCHES:

Researchers believe that climate change will make winters shorter but more brutal. The extra moisture in the air may well fuel some huge snowstorms and blizzards. Changing wind patterns may mean that cold air from the Arctic can travel further south than before, bringing blizzards to areas that wouldn't normally experience them.

TORNADOES: With more moisture in the air, storms might become more common and more intense, but it is not clear how much impact climate change will have on tornado activity.

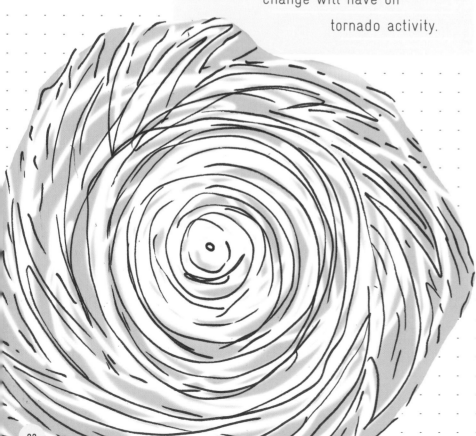

TROPICAL CYCLONES:

Scientists are not sure whether tropical cyclones will become more frequent as a result of climate change, but they do predict that they will become more intense. As ocean temperatures rise, tropical cyclones will have plenty of fuel to feed off and grow. Research indicates that hurricanes in the North Atlantic have increased in intensity over the past two decades and will continue to do so.

CLIMATE CHANGE AND GEOLOGICAL DISASTERS

It is clear how a warming climate can lead to changing weather patterns and more intense meteorological disasters, but it seems that it can also increase patterns of geological disasters.

EARTHQUAKES AND TSUNAMIS:

There are connections between extreme meteorological events and earthquakes. Earthquakes have been known to happen after big dumps of rain from hurricanes or typhoons. Scientists believe this may be because floodwaters change the pressure on the earth's crust, allowing faults to move more easily. If hurricanes do increase in intensity, there may be more earthquakes as a result.

The last time our planet experienced serious warming was at the end of the last ice age, around 15,000 years ago. Temperatures rose by 6 °C, melting great ice sheets and in doing so, releasing pressure on faults, causing a series of magnitude eight earthquakes. Dozens of giant volcanoes that had been buried under ice became active once more.

In Greenland a similar thing is happening. The ice caps are melting at a rate of around 272 billion tonnes per year. If this activates seismic faults, it may cause tsunamis to race across the North Atlantic, hitting the shores of populated areas.

VOLCANOES: At the moment, ten percent of active volcanoes are covered in ice. As that ice melts, magma will rise to the surface. In addition to this, the melting ice can cause big landslides down the slopes of the volcanoes. This can then destabilise the magma chambers and increase the likelihood of an eruption.

WHAT NEXT?

People in poorer countries are hardest hit by natural disasters. Badly constructed buildings and poor infrastructure means that the destruction is much greater, and rescue efforts are slower and harder to coordinate. Despite being the least responsible for greenhouse emissions, it is people in these countries who will suffer the most from climate change and from the extreme events that result.

The world is facing the biggest environmental challenge we have ever seen. It is a race against time to reduce greenhouse gas emissions and save our planet and all the species that exist upon it.

INDEX

Written by Robin Jacobs
Illustrated by Sophie Williams
Reference adviser: Dr. Syed Malik

British Library Cataloguing-in-
Publication Data.

A CIP record for this book is available
from the British Library.
ISBN: 978-1-908714-70-1

First published in the United Kingdom
in 2019. This edition published in 2021
Cicada Books Ltd
48 Burghley Road
London, NW5 1UE
www.cicadabooks.co.uk

© Cicada Books Limited

Printed in China